Carol,

Thank you for a wonderful time and the best pictures we've ever had taken.

Love,

Lynnette.Rios@gmail.com

Born from Love

A Single Mother by Choice

LANIA SALAS

BALBOA.PRESS
A DIVISION OF HAY HOUSE

Copyright © 2020 Lania Salas.

All rights reserved. No part of this book may be used or reproduced by any means, graphic, electronic, or mechanical, including photocopying, recording, taping or by any information storage retrieval system without the written permission of the author except in the case of brief quotations embodied in critical articles and reviews.

This book is a work of non-fiction. Unless otherwise noted, the author and the publisher make no explicit guarantees as to the accuracy of the information contained in this book and in some cases, names of people and places have been altered to protect their privacy.

Balboa Press books may be ordered through booksellers or by contacting:

Balboa Press
A Division of Hay House
1663 Liberty Drive
Bloomington, IN 47403
www.balboapress.com
1 (877) 407-4847

Because of the dynamic nature of the Internet, any web addresses or links contained in this book may have changed since publication and may no longer be valid. The views expressed in this work are solely those of the author and do not necessarily reflect the views of the publisher, and the publisher hereby disclaims any responsibility for them.

The author of this book does not dispense medical advice or prescribe the use of any technique as a form of treatment for physical, emotional, or medical problems without the advice of a physician, either directly or indirectly. The intent of the author is only to offer information of a general nature to help you in your quest for emotional and spiritual well-being. In the event you use any of the information in this book for yourself, which is your constitutional right, the author and the publisher assume no responsibility for your actions.

Any people depicted in stock imagery provided by Getty Images are models, and such images are being used for illustrative purposes only. Certain stock imagery © Getty Images.

Print information available on the last page.

ISBN: 978-1-9822-5180-2 (sc)
ISBN: 978-1-9822-5181-9 (e)

Balboa Press rev. date: 07/31/2020

DEDICATION

TO MY TWO Princes. Life with you has been my best adventure, by far.

To my Mother and Father. You gave me unconditional love and the freedom to explore the world with my own wings.

AUTHOR'S NOTE

SOME NAMES HAVE been changed to protect people's identity. In addition, nick-names have been used instead of names for some characters. The purpose of this is to help the reader keep track of multiple characters.

CONTENTS

Dedication v
Author's Note vii

Chapter 1 Ask for a Sign, Get a Signal 1
Chapter 2 Just Friends 5
Chapter 3 Reaching the Horizon 13
Chapter 4 Hiding Place 17
Chapter 5 I Can Do It On My Own 21
Chapter 6 No Perfect Boyfriend, No Perfect Donor 25
Chapter 7 Vials 35
Chapter 8 Turbulence 45
Chapter 9 White Dress 49
Chapter 10 Definitely/Maybe 55
Chapter 11 Tell Him 63
Chapter 12 Second Opinion 75
Chapter 13 The One Who Could Have Been 77
Chapter 14 Surgery 95
Chapter 15 IVF 101
Chapter 16 I Think I'm Falling 109
Chapter 17 Ultrasound 119
Chapter 18 Graduation 127
Chapter 19 Genetic Testing 131
Chapter 20 New Job 141
Chapter 21 Week 20 Ultrasound 153
Chapter 22 HELLP 157
Chapter 23 Nature's Cruel Way 167
Chapter 24 Week 33 179

Epilogue 193
Acknowledgements 197
About the Author 199

Chapter 1

ASK FOR A SIGN, GET A SIGNAL

"Please God, send me a sign. Please, please, tell me if what I'm planning is okay with you."

August 2008

THE DAY I turned 32 I woke up with the heavy feeling that I'd let another year pass me by without doing anything to make my biggest dream come true. I no longer had an excuse. I had a great career, a nice house and a good if not great savings account. I had waited one year into my new job but I was still afraid of taking that first step.

What the hell am I waiting for? I asked myself, annoyed, as I opened my eyes and stared at the ceiling, the same question I had been asking myself over and over for the last few years.

I got out of bed and after brushing my teeth I dragged myself downstairs to get my morning cup of Coke.

"Why not?" I protested to myself. "No need to give up caffeine yet." I brought my cup upstairs to my room and instead of hitting the computer, I sat on the beige carpet and grabbed the catalog that I got at the clinic. I browsed through the paperwork I had completed months before but was too chicken-shit to mail out.

It was my Friday off, so I didn't have to rush to work. My flip phone rang and I got up to grab it. I never carried my cell phone around. It was not allowed at work and God forbid I brought it in by error.

"Happy birthday, baby!" My mother beamed at the other end, making me smile for the first time that morning.

"Hey, mom. Thank you." I sipped my coke and then stopped, hoping she would not ask what I was drinking. "What are you up to?"

"I've been looking for a signal to call you, but there is no signal anywhere in this hospital."

"Hospital? What's going on?" I put my cup on my desk.

"I'm fine. Tia Lydia is getting some scans."

"Oh," I said, somewhere in the back of my mind registering that my mother's favorite aunt was having headaches and her doctor suspected it might be a tumor. I sat in front of my laptop and flipped it open. "How is Tia?"

"She's doing well. I'm here mostly to help my cousins with the medical terminology. I told them it was your birthday but I couldn't find a signal to call you, and you know who helped me?"

"Who?" I asked, opening my email.

"Padre Daniel. He came into the room when he found out Tia Lydia was here and he said, 'Come with me, I know where to find the sign.'"

"The sign?" My skin filled with goosebumps.

"Yes, *la señal*," my mom responded as if that made more sense. "Padre Daniel is now the hospital chaplain, and he knows the best place to make calls. He took me to the Virgin Mary."

My brain tried harder to keep up with my mother's tale. "So, you were able to get a signal around the statue of the Virgin Mary?"

"Yes. Father Daniel says he comes to the Virgin to make his calls," she said, laughing.

"Mom?" I asked with trepidation.

"Yes, honey?"

"Where exactly are you? What hospital?"

"Immaculate Conception, of course," she said. "The hospital where you were born."

Of course, my brain echoed. I was the only person in our hometown born 5 towns away because my mother worked there at the time.

Okay God, I get it!

After I hung up, I grabbed the catalog again and dialed the number listed on the cover.

My birthday present to myself.

Chapter 2

JUST FRIENDS

August 1999

I MET HIM at the welcome ceremony for the new bioengineering graduate students. My hands shook as I opened the conference room door. Inside was the unknown for which I had signed up, a new goal, the biggest one of my life so far. The room wasn't crowded but rather full, even though I was a few minutes early.

Maybe I'm still on Puerto Rican time, I thought.

I headed towards the table with the only familiar face, a tall blond female graduate student about a decade older than me whom I had met earlier that week at another mixer. The only three women in the entire room all wore baseball caps.

"This is Lania, a new Masters student," she said, introducing me to the people at the table and they in turn introduced themselves. I could not retain their names but I gathered they were all students.

I took the only empty chair and tried to follow the conversation. Slowly I started noting the distinguishing features of the people around me, in particular a tall, black haired guy with blue eyes who seemed as awkward as I felt. I learned he was also a new Masters student while the rest were in the Doctoral program.

"Wow!" I said. I wish I'd had the nerve to apply to the doctoral program but I didn't know how things would go, if I would get used to it or if I was PhD material. I wondered if that was also the case with the blue-eyed guy sitting next to me. He seemed intelligent but not in a geeky way. He had a cute, rather than handsome, next-door guy look.

"Why did you choose ASU?" I asked him.

"Sun Devils!" he said, raising his fist.

"What's that?"

"Really?" he asked. "You don't know Sparky and the Sun Devils?"

I shook my head.

"They're your new school's mascot."

"Oh," I didn't know what to say.

"How about you? Why did you choose ASU?"

"Because it doesn't snow in Arizona," I said and he laughed.

"Don't like snow, I take it?"

"In high school I used to walk to school with snow up to my knees," I explained. "We lived in Iowa."

"That's not where your accent is from, is it?"

"No, I'm from Puerto Rico, but my father did his PhD in Iowa, and he moved us all there with him."

"Oh," he said and looked away.

"What about your family? What do they do?"

"My parents own a ranch," he said, plainly.

The Chairman of the department interrupted the crowd to make his welcome statement, and my new friend took that opportunity to excuse himself to go grab some food. I followed him with my gaze. He had a nice athletic body.

He's trouble, I said to myself, looking down and shaking my head.

To me, he immediately became Hubbell, like the character from the movie *The Way We Were*.

My Hubbell.

More people arrived at the welcome ceremony until the room was full of students of various levels and faculty. The Chair asked the new students to think of three questions to ask to the person sitting to our right. Hubbell sat to my left. He asked me his questions, then it was my turn.

"What state are you from?"

"Montana," he answered.

I tried to think of a better question, but only one came to mind. "Do you have a girlfriend?" I asked and immediately wanted to take it back.

"Yes," he answered.

OK, that's it, I swore to myself. *I'm not making the same mistake again. Just friends.*

The next week our first semester officially began. We didn't have any classes in common but we saw each other at the grad students' office, a large classroom filled with cubicles and three computers. I used the computers to do my homework until I bought one of my own. Even then, it was less lonely to study *on campus* than in my one-bedroom apartment.

My cube was away from the door, but I memorized the sound of his steps.

"Hey there." He leaned against the wall of my cube, still wearing his sling bag and holding his water bottle in his hand.

Why, oh, why! "Did you find a roommate?"

"Yeah, we're moving in this weekend," he said. "I need to get furniture. He has a table and chairs but I need at least a sofa. Wanna come shopping with me?"

Well, I needed furniture too.

In October he came by and asked if I wanted to go with him to the Halloween party.

"Sure!"

The party was at an older house near campus, rented by three second-year ASU students. They had a keg, wine boxes, loud music and huge pumpkins. I had never carved a pumpkin and didn't feel like learning. The house was packed. I spent most of the night talking to a Pacific Islander.

Sometime later, after the crowd had scattered, we moved to the main room and I saw Hubbell sitting there, carving a pumpkin, alone. I left the Islander and walked over to him.

"Are you okay?" I asked.

He nodded without looking up.

"Wanna go?" I asked.

"Yeah, I'm ready to go."

It was dark when we headed back to his truck. My head spun as the unfamiliar roads flew by.

"Where are we going?" I asked.

"To your place," he said.

"Oh." I laughed, and I wondered if despite my sudden fear I hoped otherwise. "I think I'm tipsy."

He snorted. "Yeah, I can tell."

He was a gentleman that night. He took me home and left.

From then on we went everywhere together. We mingled, but at the end of the night we found our way to each other and stayed there.

"Here, try my beer," became a favorite game.

I didn't care for Monday Night Football, but he would call me afterwards or come over on his way home.

"It's easier to drive here than to my apartment," he said. "There's only two right turns and one left."

"Yeah, right. There's only two left turns to yours." I smiled.

We talked for hours, sitting on my new couch with our legs intertwined, or laying on my bed, side by side, staring at the roof while listening to Coldplay's *The Scientist*.

The day I bought my new computer he drove over to help me with it, but by the time he arrived I had most of it installed.

"You're pretty good with this," he said. "My girlfriend's not very tech-savvy."

I loved the compliment. "It's pretty fool-proof," I shrugged.

"I've been thinking about getting a laptop but not sure if I should get a PC or a Mac. Most computers in the lab are Macs."

"Get a PC," I advised. "You know what they say about Macs."

He shook his head. "Nope. What?"

"How do you accelerate a Mac?"

"How?"

"9.8 meters per squared second."

He laughed. "Throwing it out the window!" He got himself a PC.

After mid-terms we went to a dance club with 70's through 90's music called *Have a Nice Day Café*. He ordered what looked like a fish bowl of Kool-Aid. I tried it and found it loaded.

One of our friends introduced me to a tall, blond, blue-eyed friend of his. The blond guy spent the night telling me I was the girl of his dreams. That was the first and last night I ever saw him.

There was a new girl within our group, with long dark wavy hair. She wore a mini-skirt. Hubbell seemed familiar with her.

What happened to his girlfriend? I wondered. *But no, he would tell me.*

When I got tired of dancing I asked my new blond guy friend to walk me to my car. Before leaving, I went to let Hubbell know. I found him close to *Miniskirt*, but when he saw me, he walked over to my side. I wanted to say something but had trouble wording it.

"Behave!" I finally said.

"Behave?" he laughed and nodded.

That night I didn't get a call from him.

One night I got too drunk and our friends took my keys away and drove me home. Hubbell called me later that night.

"I wanted to make sure you got home all right," he said.

"Hold on," I said to him and ran to the bathroom. When I got back to the phone he was laughing.

"Did you just barf?"

"No, I went to powder my nose. What'd you think, silly?" I asked in a whisper and he laughed in a whisper too. Minutes later

Hubbell asked me to hold on and was away from the phone for several minutes. This was my turn to laugh.

We kept on talking in whispers. "How can you understand me?" I asked. "I can barely understand myself."

"I don't know," he whispered back. "Must be the Universal Language of Drunkenness."

We whispered through the night until we fell asleep, still holding on to our phones.

We didn't talk much during finals, until he decided to take a break from studying and came for a visit. The early December weather still felt warm in Arizona, so we sat outside on a small patch of over-manicured grass in front of my apartment. We sat side by side, staring out at the orange and blue desert sunset.

"Can you believe he had the nerve to email me?" I complained. "Why'd he do that?"

"Dunno," he shrugged. "But you still have feelings for him and you didn't need this during finals."

He got me, but what he didn't know was those old feelings were fading.

"Do you remember the dark-haired girl I was talking to the night we went dancing?"

I had an immediate flashback to the fish bowls, the brunette with the miniskirt and the close dancing. "What about her?"

"Well, I broke up with my girlfriend, and I'm kind of seeing her."

My jaw dropped. *Just friends.*

"I got a bit too drunk," he explained, "so she drove me home and spent the night with me." Then at my blank stare he added, "but nothing happened."

Yeah, I knew about *nothing happening*. You could spend all night doing *nothing*.

I wish things had stayed that way, just friends. I wish the chapter had ended right then and there, but it didn't.

Or maybe I don't wish for that at all. Life is too short to regret the fun we had.

Either way, if I had learned my lesson this time around, it would have looked like the most basic of mathematical equations:

$$1 + 1 = 2$$
$$1 + 1 + n \neq 2,$$

where n is an integer ≥ 1

Since I refused to acknowledge the equation, I had to repeat this course a couple more times before grasping its full meaning. Once learned, the Heavens applauded, and I finally passed on to the next level.

Chapter 3

REACHING THE HORIZON

May 2005

MY GRAD SCHOOL advisor encouraged me to do a postdoc after graduation. I felt honored to be considered for such a position, until I told my parents and my mother had a fit.

"No! You can't keep on going! You have to stop at some point and get married. If you wait too long you will regret it."

True, but she didn't know what it was like, she had only dated once.

Arizona had been the ideal lifestyle, because I knew I was moving forward in life. I partied almost every night, I dated, I danced, I traveled to international conferences and I visited friends. I had the time of my life. After Hubbell, I met a group of international students who loved road trips as much as I did, and with them I lived life's adventures. I went camping to Strawberry, Arizona, where going to the bathroom means going behind a cactus. I decided from then on I would stick to cabin-camping or camping at the nearest Best Western. I drove to Rocky Point, Mexico on the spur of the moment and had to sleep in the car, in front of the border because none of us knew they closed the gates at midnight. When the gates opened the next morning, we drove on to the beach. We rented a houseboat and sailed along Lake Powell. The views were breathtaking. Talking about views, my friends hiked the Grand Canyon while I hiked all the souvenir stores. I traveled to Chile, to reunite with my teenage best friend and pen pal for life, Barbie, before she gave birth to her first son. I went to conferences and toured Washington DC, New Orleans, California, Seattle, North Carolina and various other states. At home in Arizona, I knew the best places for dancing in Phoenix and Scottsdale for each day of the week.

Eventually, six Arizona summers began to burn down my spirits.

I stopped going out and focused on my dissertation. I focused so much that I finished it in three months. After graduation I had that huge feeling of relief, no pressure, no responsibilities.

"And now what?"

"A postdoc," my advisor insisted during every conference he took me to, the same way he had proposed the Doctorate when I was about to finish my Masters. I looked at postdoctoral programs at different universities, but I felt tired. I would be turning 30 that fall. This was not something I could explain to my advisor no matter how insistent he was.

"I don't like the postdoctoral salary," I said instead, moving from research poster to poster while he continued talking next to me.

"I can help you get a scholarship," he offered, then he made me promise I would consider it.

I thought about my goals. I had friends who had wanted to marry right after high school. Not me! I dreaded the idea of being tied to a husband, a house and a daily routine. Now my 20's were nearly over, and I felt ready to move on towards something more permanent.

I interviewed in industry, the engineering equivalent of a corporate job, but I found the jobs and the cities highly depressing. When I first applied to ASU, I wrote on my essay,

I want to reach the horizon.

NASA came to mind. As a teen that had been my ultimate goal. I looked into postdoctoral programs at NASA and I started feeling better about the whole concept. There was a particular research that caught my attention, a lab-on-a-chip device, but the Principal Investigator wasn't from NASA. He was from The National Laboratories.

"Yeah, right, who is going to accept me at The National Labs?" I thought. The place that invented the atomic bomb was highly selective and I had not graduated Ivy League with a 4.00 grade average, I had struggled through most of my studies.

Still, the idea intrigued me. The Labs were supported by government agencies and had the highest tech equipment anyone could hope to work with. The next time my advisor brought up the subject I firmly stated,

"The only way I will do a postdoc is if it's at The National Labs."

My advisor and God seem to share the same sense of humor. My advisor made a call and a few weeks later I had an interview at The National Labs.

I learned that when something is meant to be, you take the first step, then the universe propels you forward.

Chapter 4

HIDING PLACE

Summer 2009

"DID YOU TRY to become a mother before you came to live here?" my lawyer asked.

"No," I answered. "I have known that I was willing to be a single mother since I was ten," I responded, and my lawyer seemed surprised, "but no, it all started when I moved to Albuquerque."

Summer 2006

When you move to a new city, you need to find the first essentials: a place to live, your way around new roads, a good supermarket, a new church and the nearest hospital, just in case. Because I am a woman and I am me, I also needed to find a new OB/Gyn, so I made the dreaded appointment.

I was glad to discover my new OB/Gyn was a tall lady with gray hair tied up in a bun. She wore a long colorful skirt and sandals.

A hippie, I thought.

She sat across from me at her office, chair in front of chair, chart in hand.

"When was your last period?"

I never remembered so I guesstimated, plus or minus a few weeks, and she wrote it down as fact.

She continued with her questionnaire and when she was satisfied she placed the chart on her lap and smiled directly at me. "So what brings you to Albuquerque?"

"I was offered a postdoc at The National Labs."

"Ooh, impressive!" she said, her eyes opening wide. "I have a lot of patients whose husbands work at The Labs."

Yeah, husbands, I thought. *Not a single patient who works there, I bet.* I smiled while waiting for the next question. I really wanted to get the conversation done with. I wanted my prescription and to go home. She must have read my mind.

"You said you use Toradol, right?" she said flipping back through her chart.

"Yes, 2cc's."

"You mean 20 milligrams, right?" she asked sweetly.

"No, I inject myself."

"That sounds serious," she said, looking at me again. "Why don't you take it orally?"

The office felt cold. I wanted to brace myself. "Because the pain makes me vomit and it turns into a positive feedback loop."

"You should take contraceptives."

"Oh, no," I shook my head decisively. "I used them during grad school but then I stopped," I answered as I rubbed my hands together to warm them up.

"It would help you regulate all those symptoms."

"I just want to be able to get to work, instead of missing work for three days every month," I assured her, and she nodded, understanding.

"You could try one with low estrogen. I can help you choose a good brand."

I took a deep breath. How could I explain it to this nice lady? I looked at her and she looked back, expectantly.

"I don't want contraceptives because I want to be able to have a child instead of preventing it, even if it means doing it on my own." I blurted it all out in a single breath, and then I couldn't inhale. I fought hard to keep my face calm, to keep my best professional poker face, but I could feel hot itchy moisture filling my eyes. I had never spoken those words out loud, not even to myself.

I wanted to rub my eyes but that would make it more obvious, so I forced my hands to stay where they were, frozen. Meanwhile, she stared at me open-mouthed.

"Oh," she said, clasping her hands. "Oh!" she repeated more enthusiastically. "I get it! You are a young professional woman who has no need to wait for anyone else."

I finally breathed again.

She padded her hands up and down on her lap, then reached over the desk for a prescription pad and wrote something on it.

Finally, I thought, *I can get out of here.*

"I have a friend who is a fertility specialist, I'm going to refer you to him."

I felt the blood drain down my face. "Oh, no. No, no. I'm not ready, I didn't mean now."

"It's okay. You can get an appointment and ask all your questions!" She ripped off the prescription-referral and handed it over to me. I reached for it and held it between two fingers, staring at it without reading it. I could not, for the life of me, look at her face again.

"Let me know how it goes," she stood up and left the room to give me time to change.

As soon as she was out the door, I folded the paper into tiny squares. I didn't know what to do with it. What if it fell out of my pocket at work and my new boss figured out what I was up to? Or worse, what if I put it in my wallet and my mother discovered it while getting some cash?

I placed the paper in the cell phone pocket of my purse and closed the zipper tight.

I walked around with the piece of paper in my purse for half a year before I had the nerve to take it out. When I did, I looked at the wrinkled piece of paper, a bit torn at the edges, and asked myself the question I always ask before making any big decisions:

What will I regret more, doing it or not doing it?

In this case, not doing it was not an option.

Chapter 5

I CAN DO IT ON MY OWN

September 2008

- ✓ Papers mailed to cryobank
- ✓ Fertility tests completed
- − Donor chosen *(narrowing down)*
- − Mind at ease…

I WENT TO the last required appointment with my Reproductive Endocrinologist (RE) with a huge list of questions. He laughed. He didn't laugh often, or smile, but he said I cracked him up.

"You are so analytical," he said, and I took it as a compliment. He sat behind a large mahogany desk, wearing a long white lab coat, his head bald and shiny. I sat in front of his desk like a grade school girl at the Principal's office. I seemed to be his youngest patient. Most other women in the waiting area were either in their mid to late 40's with serious executive husbands next to them, or slightly younger, sometimes overweight women accompanied by a female partner. I had just turned 32, petite, with a minimum of gray hair on my brown mane and normally wore jeans, even to work. No one at The Labs overdressed because we would wear lab coats over our clothes. I tried to set up my medical appointments first thing in the mornings, before the clinic opened. That way I could get the appointment over with and arrive at work at a decent time.

I asked my RE if any of his patients had ever regretted this decision.

"No," he answered. "They look happy every time they bring back their children for me to meet."

I openly asked if he had any recommendations for me.

"I need to question your decision because girls, women, that look like you have a good chance of getting married."

That sounded nice, but he had no idea.

To sum it up, among regular people I was a nerd, but among nerds I guess I was considered "cute like a doll," as a boy once told me in high school, and I had gotten angry thinking it was a reference to my height.

Then there were the others. In grad school, I found out that both of Hubbell's roommates wanted to date me.

"Why do they like me?" I asked Hubbell.

"Why wouldn't they? You're nice, pretty and smart," he replied.

Still, I did not want to discuss my dating history with my doctor, so I kept silent through this particular lecture, nodding as required.

"I understand it might not be easy to form a relationship. Even my 25-year-old son tells me how frustrating it is to find the right girl," my doctor continued.

Why don't you set me up with your son? I thought.

"Do you have any more questions for me?" he asked, sensing he hadn't changed my mind.

"Yes." I still had my biggest question, the one I'd come here to ask, left unchecked on my list. I didn't have to look down at my notes to remember this one.

"Am I rushing this?"

Most of my tests were good. I had plenty of eggs left and they seemed viable, but my estrogen levels were high which could be a sign of early menopause, something I suspected would happen to me, since I had had my first period two months after turning ten.

My doctor did not smile this time. In a professional voice he answered,

"No. Definitely not. Most women think they have until their 40's to get started but that is not the case at all. Fertility in a woman starts to decline around your age and declines even faster in the following years. The older patients I see often have problems conceiving or they have to use donor egg to become pregnant."

He brought out a chart of fertility versus treatment. It showed that women undergoing fertility treatment had their best chance of becoming pregnant by their third attempt. If they were not pregnant at that point, their chances would decrease with every subsequent attempt and neared zero after the 5th attempt. The graph was engraved in my brain.

I finally had all the information I needed. After leaving his office, I completed the rest of the required paperwork and set up an appointment for the day of my approaching ovulation cycle, the following week.

Back home I only had one task left to complete. I needed to choose a donor.

Chapter 6

NO PERFECT BOYFRIEND, NO PERFECT DONOR

"IF YOU ARE going to have a child, why can't you just, you know, enjoy making it?"

"It depends," I answered my *comadre's* question. She and I had been high school friends, college roommates and then I became her son's Godmother. "Some guys do a good job, but others don't."

She remained quiet and I wondered why.

"Besides, it's fun to choose. I get to pick what I like."

I had narrowed down my choices to three, but I was not sharing this fact with her. While she always trusted me with her personal issues, I didn't feel inclined to do the same. Not that she wasn't trustworthy but she was very close to her cousins, who had also been my college housemates, and they belonged to a large family from a small town, my hometown, where the main source of information was still gossip. Much faster and less reliable than Facebook or Twitter. My friend and I were related by marriage, her aunt, my uncle. So no, this information was mine.

At one point, when Hubbell got back together with his ex, my *comadre* introduced me to a guy from our hometown. His name was Oscar. It was at a Christmas party. My *comadre* smiled from ear to ear as Oscar and I seemed to hit it off. In early January, Oscar called me in Arizona and we got together. We went hiking, then he invited me to a nice restaurant for Valentine's. We saw each other often that Spring. One Saturday evening we went to a movie, then I cooked for him at home and we had a late dinner. He left my apartment close to midnight.

The next morning it was my aunt's birthday, so I called her in Puerto Rico to wish her a happy birthday.

"I heard you cooked for Oscar last night," she said. "He told his mother you make the most delicious white rice he's ever had."

Oscar's jaw dropped when I repeated my aunt's conversation to him. That didn't turn out to be an isolated event. He invited me on a weekend trip to Las Vegas. Initially, I said yes, but then I wondered how Abuela would take the news at church on Sunday, so I canceled at the last minute. He went by himself and met with a friend there. A guy, supposedly. When he returned, he jokingly asked,

"So what have you heard about my trip?"

"Ha!" I said. "No reports on who you really spent the weekend with, but you went to a Puerto Rican restaurant and the white rice was nowhere as delicious as mine."

Once again his jaw dropped.

From then on, we became very cautious about what we told each other.

"Don't tell anyone!"

I couldn't tell anyone why Oscar started using my car while he shopped around for a new BMW (he crashed his car). He couldn't tell anyone I had downed a triple shot of Tequila (like it was water). He definitely couldn't tell anyone I usually hung out with a dozen guys, all Bioengineers (all those *Machos*).

It got to be too much when my young cousins started spying on me. They would call my apartment, which was the same number as my cell phone. If they heard voices (when I was on campus) they would tell Abuela they heard voices, maybe Oscar, in my apartment (God forbid).

"There's something missing between the two of you," Hubbell pointed out when he met Oscar for the first time.

Honestly, gossip wasn't what came between Oscar and me.

What came between us was Hubbell in my apartment every night after I said goodnight to Oscar, and before Oscar's call in the morning.

So no, I could not confide in my *comadre* my choice of donor. I had to do this on my own. I wasn't sharing what donor I chose, not even with my mother.

Mainly, my biggest consideration was to my future child. I wanted a healthy donor, but I also wanted him to be smart and cute. I wanted a donor willing to meet my child. I was adamant I needed to provide this opportunity for my child. Some donors at California Cryobank were Open Donors, which meant the donor could be contacted when the child turned 18. Their sperm was more expensive but I saw it as an essential expense.

I tried to visualize a future meeting between this person and my child. I imagined a young man in his late teens. I decided to shift the image to a young lady. She met her for the first time at a coffee shop and both chose to sit outside.

What would they talk about?

They needed to have things in common, like hobbies, so it made sense if the donor had some of the same hobbies I had, like writing. I didn't want my child to feel rejected for things like religion or ethnicity, so I searched for a donor with Catholic or at least Christian background, since I planned to raise my child in my faith. If the donor wasn't Hispanic, he would have to at least have studied Spanish in high school or have lived in a Spanish-speaking country.

With a huge decision like this, I wished I had a trustworthy friend I could talk to, but my closest friends were coworkers at *The Labs*. My good friends were long distance friends, courtesy of my moving around so much for school and jobs, and my father's career before that.

I had learned about a group of Single Mothers by Choice after reading a NY Times article but I hadn't joined their group yet.

They had a $50 fee to become a member, which I could pay, but it felt pretentious to assume I would be one of them. I didn't want to jinx it. Instead, I emailed the one person in the world I could always trust. It didn't matter if Barbie told other people because I would never meet them. We lived on different continents.

Hi Barbie, I began my email, like always. Barbie was my best friend during our first year of high school in Iowa, but when the year was over she went back to Chile, and years later, my family went back to Puerto Rico. It hurt to say goodbye, not knowing if I would ever see her again, but then God created the internet.

> *Hi Barbie.*
>
> *I have two great candidates. I am attaching their baby pictures. The one with dark hair is half Jewish and half Latino, goes to graduate school, did well in his SAT's and has a good family health history, except for an aunt with diabetes. Must be the Hispanic side, I have that in my family too. What I don't like is that he wrote that his father is in jail.*
>
> *The blond one is nearly perfect, great at school and great in sports. I only have his baby picture but I think he must be gorgeous. He has French and German ancestors, takes daily vitamins but unfortunately has also taken recreational cannabis for the last five years. I don't want to support his habit! What do you think? Could you help me decide?*
>
> *Hugs,*
> *Lania*

I opened Facebook to stay distracted while I waited for an answer. The problem was that because of her two young children I sometimes had to wait several days. Not that I should complain.

It was so much harder before we discovered email. We spent years writing letters to each other. Although we answered a letter immediately, each letter took two weeks to get delivered from Chile to Iowa, or Puerto Rico, so we could only count on monthly communications. Often, by the time she responded to my letter and I received it, the problem I had mentioned in my letter was not an issue anymore.

The best thing about Barbie, though, was that she was always there, like a guardian angel, day and night. When I needed her I only had to reach for pen and paper or for my computer. Years ago, when we were teenagers, I blamed God when we had to part ways but God had a purpose, even if it took years, or decades, for it to unravel. I read somewhere that life was easy to understand when you look back, but you still have to live it forward.

Facebook didn't help me stay distracted. I got up to grab something to eat when I heard the instant messenger bell.

Forget food! I clicked on her picture and immediately it was like seeing her face-to-face.

"Who cares!" she wrote on the first line. You are not marrying these guys!!!"

"But what if the drug overuse causes some sort of deformity on my child?"

"Don't choose that one, I like the dark-haired one better, anyway." It took her a long time to write and send each line. It made me think she was breastfeeding her baby girl and typing with only one hand, like the last time we video chatted.

"What about the donor's father?" I asked her and waited.

"That's the father, not him."

"What if my child inherits a weird psychotic gene? Or what if my child wants to meet those people some day?"

"I don't know. Can you choose someone else? How did you find their baby pictures?"

"They posted them on the cryobank website."

"Really? Can I search too?"

"Anyone can, but you have to pay a separate fee for the baby pictures."

"Fuck them!"

"Lol! Here," I wrote. I opened a new tab on my browser and copy and pasted the link to her.

I had found California Cryobank by googling *cryobank*. I should have known that was like googling the word *aspirin* expecting to come up with the most ethical pharmaceutical, but my knowledge of cryobanks was very limited back then and I had no one to turn to for advice. The two articles I had read mostly focused on the relationships of single women before and after deciding to become single mothers. Moreover, my internet searches were done in the privacy of my own home, much like a young teen searching for porn.

"What are you looking for?" came the new message from Barbie. "Health, I suppose."

"Yes, that's the most important thing, but you have to screen them by the characteristics on the left of the webpage first. There's height, eye color," I wrote.

"I see it. I suppose you want blue eyes," she stated more than asked.

"Of course," I admitted. *My weakness.*

"What else? Tall?"

"Yeah, but I don't write anything there. I don't want to rule them out because of height just yet."

"Ethnicity?"

"I like Asians, and mixed, but I prefer Hispanic."

"Is that all?" Barbie asked.

"Let's choose religion."

"Are you serious?"

"If we were Jewish, would you question me?"

"No," she admitted, "but you should be open to other options, not just Catholics."

"I'm choosing Christian."

"And why is that important?"

"Because," I typed but had to think about it. "Just because my religion is important to *me*." I sent out that part of the message but I knew there was more to it. "And just in case my child wants to meet him one day, so they will have something basic in common."

"Ok, then, religion, Christian, marked. Are you going to choose an Area of Study?"

"No."

"I don't believe it." She must have put her baby in her crib because her answers came faster.

"I will choose an Engineer over a Musician, but I can decide later, or I won't come up with any choices."

"Genius," she wrote sarcastically.

"Blood type?"

"I don't care, leave that blank."

"What is *Donor Type*? Choices are, *Anonymous* and *Open*."

"Open," I answered. "So my child can contact him after turning 18," I answered.

"OPEN" we both wrote at the same time.

We came up with several choices out of over five-hundred available donors.

"Oh, look, the third one is an engineer."

"We can discard that one," I typed. "He's the druggie."

"What do you look for next? I want to see the pictures."

"Some of them don't have pictures, so I can discard those. Now I read their profiles and their health information," I answered. Barbie stopped typing and I could tell she was engrossed in reading.

"They all have something," she typed and added a sad face.

"No perfect boyfriend, no perfect donor," I told her.

"Speak for yourself. I have a great husband."

"He is pretty great," I sighed. "Tell me something. If you had written a letter to God with all the characteristics you wanted in a husband, would that be him?"

"Yes, I think so," she answered, "I had never thought about it that way, but yes, he is what I always wanted."

If I wait more, maybe I will also get what I want, I thought. Then I remembered the list I wrote in my last year of grad school. "I like the Biologist."

"Which one is that?" Barbie typed. "Never mind, I found him."

She was silent for a bit and so was I.

"He has a PhD!" she wrote.

"Yeah, and seasonal allergies," I wrote back.

"Is that okay?" she asked.

"All things considered, I guess it's not horrible."

"So why are you hesitant?" Barbie asked.

"When I first saw him, there were no reported pregnancies, now his profile says he has proven pregnancies."

"And that's good or bad?"

"Depends. For someone who wants proof that her donor is fertile, that might be good news."

"But not for you. How come?"

"It also means he already has donor children out there, that another woman has used this donor. It feels odd. I could never stand a boyfriend cheating on me. I don't like the idea of my guy having God knows how many women out there pregnant."

"*Chucha!*" I could almost hear her exclaim it. "I wouldn't like that either. So where does that leave us? Another guy?"

"I don't know. This might not be something I can control. Before me or after me, the bank will keep on selling his sperm, so there will be other children from other women."

"True," Barbie responded. "Are you willing to consider this one, then?"

"Maybe. I could at least see what he looks like."

"How can you do that?"

"Let me purchase his baby picture." I went to get my wallet and entered my credit card information. In a matter of minutes, I was able to open a picture that looked like it had been taken in the 70's, of a cute little blond boy standing on a green lawn, wearing red shorts and a striped t-shirt. I immediately sent it to Barbie.

"Awww, he's so cute," Barbie wrote. "He looks a little bit geeky."

"Yes," I agreed, staring at the picture on my end. "I'm gonna get him."

Chapter 7

VIALS

I CALLED THE cryobank the morning of my birthday but they wanted the paperwork I had not sent yet. It took me a few more days to place the order. The staff at my fertility clinic were happy to help me send the paperwork and called the cryobank directly to place the order.

"How many vials of sperm would you like to order?" the patient coordinator asked me while holding the phone between her shoulder and ear.

My face turned hot as I had to ask her. "How many will I need?"

She seemed used to the question. "One for every time you plan to try to get pregnant. I would buy more than one if you like this donor."

I quickly did the math in my head. Each vial was approximately $500 (at the time), and although my health insurance covered fertility treatments, I had no proof of infertility, until I learned otherwise. I had never tried to get pregnant before. Just the opposite, I faithfully or unfaithfully avoided it. So far, I'd only had a single false alarm. That meant the cost of treatments would come out of my pocket unless there was a reason to question my fertility.

The cost of a single vial seemed affordable. I could buy one per month and still remain within my spending budget. Although if I wanted to buy a few at once it would have to come out of savings. I decided to use my credit card. It wouldn't take long to pay it off.

"I will buy three vials," I answered. That sounded like enough. With the help of ovulation tests and ultrasounds I should get pregnant with the first attempt, right?

Three sounded reasonable to the lady helping me with the order. I went to the drugstore on my way home and bought a large package of ovulation tests. I had to start testing five days before my expected ovulation date, then call the clinic to make an appointment when the test produced a dark pink line, as instructed.

Three days later, the same lady called me to let me know my order had arrived and was being stored at the clinic. I had already begun testing, and according to the light pink line on the test my first insemination was only a couple of days away. I kept testing every morning right after waking up until the pink line was as pink as I thought it could get. Then I called the doctor's office and they gave me an appointment for the very next day.

The day of the insemination I woke up extra early to make it to the doctor's office before anyone else, hoping to be out of there and back at work before anyone noticed what I was up to. I had to wait outside the clinic for the receptionist to open. Another lady walked in at the same time I did. As we were giving our information to the receptionist, another couple arrived. I sat in the waiting area and grabbed a Home Décor magazine. The nurses began arriving and the voices filled the office. I lay down the magazine and the lady who came in after me picked it up. I guessed her to be in her 40's, at least a decade older than me, and she was alone. I wanted to ask what her situation was, but it seemed intrusive. She kept on turning magazine pages and whistled when she came upon the picture of a formal sitting room with a white fireplace. I looked at her and smiled.

"Beautiful," I commented.

"I hate these magazines," she confided. "They make me feel poor."

I quietly laughed with her. She didn't look anywhere near poor, her clothes, her purse, the fact that she was a patient at a fertility clinic, but I understood her meaning. The sitting room picture in the magazine looked like it belonged at a palace, not in a suburban house, no matter how big that house was. Even my classical decorating style in my cute townhome didn't look that fancy. We waited in silence the rest of the time, until different nurses called our first names from different doors that led to opposite sides of the clinic.

My nurse led me to a medium size doctor's office, with two patient chairs, a round chair in front of a computer desk and an examination table. The nurse was all smiles as she explained that I should undress from the waist down and cover myself with a patient's wrap skirt. Alone in the room, I did as was told and lay down on the table/bed. The walls were covered with anatomy posters of the ovulation cycle and other fertility information. What held my attention was a poster displayed on the ceiling, of a man dressed in jeans, holding a newborn baby on his bare six-pack chest.

"Perfect!"

A small knock on the door indicated it was time for the procedure.

"Come in," I murmured.

Instead of the doctor, a nurse dressed in long skirts and knee-high boots walked into the room. She was the epitome of beauty and sweetness. A friend of mine who later used the same clinic and I nicknamed her *Miss America*.

"Will the doctor be performing the procedure?" I asked.

"We are all trained to do the procedure," she said in her whispery voice, and I concluded she meant the nurses. "The doctor oversees the patient's appointments and tests, but I can call him in if you have any questions. Would you like me to see if he is available now?"

I thought about the extra wait time it would take which could make me late for work. "No, I think I know what to expect."

She then asked for my license or photo ID. I reached out for my purse and showed her my recently acquired New Mexico State license. She then asked me to provide my donor's identification number, which I had been told to memorize. A second nurse brought in a vial with the color sticker I had chosen before getting into the examination room. She showed me the vial and asked me to read the donor ID number on the vial. I recited the number again and Miss America verified it was the same as written on my patient chart. She read the information on the paperwork that the second nurse had brought in with the vial. The information included the number of viable sperm and the motility of the sample, and from her assertion I understood they were good numbers, but I made a mental note to google what kind of numbers I should expect for a future visit.

The procedure was similar to a Pap exam, except that instead of taking a sample of my tissue, the sperm sample was inserted with an elongated plastic Pasteur pipette. When she was done she discarded the used tools in a biohazard bag. She asked me if I wanted to keep the empty sperm vial. I thought about it and decided I didn't want it at home. By then my brother had moved in with me and I wouldn't know where to store an empty sperm tube. My brother was one of multiple family members who didn't approve of what I was doing, so instead of providing details, I kept all information to myself.

I traveled to attend a Bioengineering conference during the dreaded two week wait (2ww) so I packed a box of pregnancy tests to use the day after my expected period. The five-day travel helped to keep my mind occupied. I knew I would encounter old friends from my Alma Mater. I felt more nervous about the prospect of possibly seeing Hubble than the possible test results. I was right about meeting many if not most of my fellow students but apparently, Hubble hadn't attended the conference. I did meet my only female professor, the one who had given birth to her first child during her postdoc, and she was impressed with my choice of postdoctoral experience.

"You're at The Labs? You're going to be very well set up for your career."

Her comment made my trip.

I also had a non-bioengineering friend from Arizona, Annie, join me for the weekend and once she arrived every free minute was spent touring Los Angeles. The conference was being held at the Loews Hotel, which wasn't the fanciest hotel I've stayed in but with the Hollywood mountain in plain view from the hallway and the Red Carpet Dolby Theater adjacent to it, it was definitely the most interesting one. I only had to walk down the stairs to tour The Walk of Fame.

Two more friends from ASU joined us for dinner at the hotel, then we walked down to the Walk of Fame in search of our favorite artists. I placed my hands over Marilyn Monroe's and got my picture taken with Ricky Martin's star. I thought Ricky's star would be barely dry since it had been inaugurated days before my trip. I wished so much I could have been there for that event. My friends and I came upon a lounge bed made of plaster. I took my shoes off and hopped on for a picture and my girlfriends followed. I felt carefree and vibrant.

Back at the hotel that night I showed my friend Annie the box of pregnancy tests.

"You did it?" she questioned in surprise.

I nodded.

"When?"

"Two weeks ago."

"You mean, you got *that thing* in you?"

"Inseminated? Yes."

"You're crazy!"

I knew to expect that reaction from her. After all, we met and became friends at church. Catholic church, plus her family tended to be as traditional or even more than mine. I put the box back in my carry-on.

"Don't you think you're being selfish?" Annie asked.

"Am I? Why?" There were so many reasons why people had children, to get a guy to propose, to keep a marriage from failing, because of a careless night.

"Maybe you expect the child to be thankful, or you're doing this so you're not lonely."

"I'm not lonely, Ann. I'm independent and happy. I don't expect the child to be thankful, that's up to the child. I want to love my child and I think I have a lot to offer."

Annie took a deep breath, her long black hair fell over her shoulders. "Never mind. I know you. I know you're doing it from a place of love."

"I am," I agreed. I had no doubt about that.

"So when will you know?"

"I'm supposed to test tomorrow."

"Oh," she looked at me, her eyes wide open. "Test now!"

I smiled eagerly. "It might be too early."

"You can test again tomorrow!"

She was right, I had a box of three tests for that same reason. I went into the bathroom and peed on one of the sticks. I washed my hands thoroughly and brought the test out of the bathroom to show her while we waited a whole minute.

One pink line.

BFN = Big Fat Negative.

I tried again a month later. Once again I had to travel while on my 2ww and once again I got a BFN. My third try was in December and I would know the result right before Christmas. This time I traveled to Puerto Rico, just like every year to spend the holidays at home with my family. I tested right before departing. Too early. I tested again a few days after I got there. Only a single pink line. I bore my disappointment alone for a couple of days, then I decided to confide in my mother.

I found her on her bed, watching TV and so I sat at the edge of her bed. She gave me a curious smile.

"Remember that talk with you and Dad over the summer?" I asked.

She sat up in bed, full attention on me. "About?"

"Yes," I replied.

"Did you do it?"

"Yes. Three times."

She pressed PAUSE on the TV and leaned back on her pillow, looking away.

My Mom and Dad had traveled to Albuquerque to spend the summer with me and my brother. That was the summer before my 31st birthday and I felt it was time to have "the talk" with them. From the time I was 12 years old, their one and only advice when I had a big decision was, "Whatever you want," but they always had my back and I felt it was important to at least give them a heads up. I wanted to have their blessing.

As always, I started the conversation with my mother. For years my mother felt the need to poke me about moving forward with my love life. She loved to know whom I was dating and all the details I was willing to share, but it also frustrated her that I wasn't getting serious with anyone. As the proud mother she was, she couldn't see any reason why I was still single other than my choice to be an engineer and to continue on to graduate school.

"Men will be scared of you," she warned.

One summer after things had ended with Hubbell and I was in the dating game again but not getting serious, she fumed that she was going to fix my love life by placing a sign on my back that read, "Single."

My decision to have "the talk" shouldn't have been a surprise. I had hinted about this possibility throughout my life.

"I'm going to be a single mother," I had often warned since I was in my teens, but I didn't have a definite method of doing it. I sort of thought it depended on who I was with at the time.

Her usual answer was, "You will be a mother when you have a father to give your child," but other times she thought it was hilarious and would boast to her friends about it rolling her eyes. "She says she's going to be a single mother."

When I seriously broached the subject with her at my dining room table, she had one foot on "when you get married" and one on "it is about time you thought about your future." In fact, she said both, with her final word being, "Well, tell your father, so he knows this is coming from you and not an idea that I'm putting in your head."

So I called my father and asked him to sit with us at the table. I had an idea of what my father would say. He had given me a clue a few years ago, the first time he had gone to visit me in Arizona so I would not spend my first Thanksgiving alone. We'd sat back then at a smaller table I had gotten from Kmart, and he was describing his clinical work at the University of Memphis.

"So many young girls come to the clinic wanting to have an abortion, while good girls like you are eager to be a mother," my father had said, deep in thought. "When your time comes, you decide whatever way works best for you."

I sat immobile with tears forming in the back of my eyes.

Even with that thought in mind, I still felt trepidation about broaching the subject of what decision would work best for me. It was one thing to jump around the subject with my mother, but with my father I had never directly played with the words, "I'm going to be a single mother."

I went upstairs to find him and asked him to come down to talk. In this new house I had a French-style glass-topped-round table. My father folded his hands on top of the glass and waited. He looked first at my mother then at me.

"I went to see a fertility specialist. I wanted to know how much time I had, how long I could wait. He had some tests done and my estrogen was a bit elevated, which could be a sign of an early cycle or of early menopause."

I can't say what my father's reaction was because I felt too embarrassed to face him. "I told the doctor I was considering insemination and asked him if I was rushing into things. He said no." I explained a bit more about my doctor's visit and my interest in having children by myself, then asked his opinion.

My father's answer also sounded like he was grasping for the right words to use. He first agreed with the doctor's conclusion. "I'm just concerned that you don't have a permanent job."

"Most women I have talked to say the best time for them to have their children was during their postdocs," I said and he nodded.

We didn't seem to have much to say, so I asked him directly, "If I want to go ahead with this, would you support my decision?"

"Absolutely," he said smiling and it was such a big relief for me.

Dad's acceptance had also seemed to satisfy my mother's anxiety, that is, until I informed her I had actually started the process.

"Why didn't you tell me?" she scolded. She grabbed the remote and this time turned off the TV.

"I did. This summer."

"But you didn't say you had started."

"I wanted to wait and see if it would work."

"Has it? Are you pregnant?" She sat forward in bed.

"No, no. I have tried three times. No pregnancy."

"Hmm. Miscarriage."

"No, Mom, no pregnancy."

"How do you know?"

"My hormone levels haven't changed. No sign of pregnancy at all."

"I need to talk to that doctor of yours," she said, as if that would fix things.

"Don't you dare!"

I drank all the rum my grandpa and uncles offered me that Christmas and New Year's Eve.

Chapter 8

TURBULENCE

AFTER THE HOLIDAYS, my brother and I flew back to Albuquerque in early January. It was the scariest, most turbulent flight of our lives. The turbulence lasted more than an hour. My brother held my hand tight through it. I could tell he was asking forgiveness for all his sins.

My parents will wake up tomorrow without children.

It didn't seem possible for the wings to withstand such harsh constant pressure. The plane kept dipping down and down, as the pilot searched for lower pressure without succeeding. It felt as if we were falling into a void, with no wind and no force holding the plane up at all.

I closed my eyes. Please, God, send your angels to hold up the wings and lead us to safety.

I visualized the plane landing safely, but a look out the windows gave me the chills. In the darkness, all that was visible were the snowy mountain peaks.

Even if the pilot lands the plane, we won't survive the night in this weather.

Finally, a clear thought entered my mind.

Pressures are low at sea level. By the time the plane dips low enough, the turbulence will subside and the pilot will have time to regain control of the plane.

I calmed down but looking around it was obvious I was the only calm person. The passengers held on tightly to their seats. I wondered how much longer it would take for the oxygen masks to come down.

No oxygen masks yet. That's a good sign, right?

I looked back to the tail of the plane and realized the flight attendants were scared too.

I was right. After a few more sudden dips, the turbulence subsided. When the plane landed, I heard one of the flight attendants say to a passenger,

"We haven't had turbulence like this in over five years."

The two weeks I spent in Puerto Rico meant I had lost my chance for a 4th cycle in January, but that was okay. I needed a break. The best part about that break was that I was eager to start again. I had used up my 3 sperm vials so I needed to order more in time for my next cycle. I went to my doctor's office and signed paperwork to order three more vials. The next day I got a call from the clinic. My donor had stopped donating. No more of his vials were being sold. I needed to choose another donor.

"Are you serious?" I asked them. "I really liked that donor."

"He retired from the program," she assured me.

But it's so hard to find one I like. I wanted to keep on wining.

I went back to the drawing board, or in this case, to the online catalogue. I did not find another PhD Biologist. No PhD's at all. I once again came up with my previous choices, the one with the father in prison and the cannabis user but by then, they both had proven pregnancies. I knew it was inevitable that there were other children, unless I could buy all the sperm vials, but I had no idea how many vials the cryobank had, or how expensive it could get to buy all of them.

Next!

I went over the available donors again and again but I didn't find one I liked. *No perfect boyfriend, no perfect donor.* I re-considered an Unknown donor but once again I rejected the idea.

What if my child wants to meet him one day?

I wanted a donor who would be willing to meet my child. I was sure about that.

I settled for a tall guy with no link to Spanish and no graduate degree. I completed the paperwork and brought it back to the clinic.

"How many vials would you like to get?" the receptionist asked me.

"Two or three," I said, and provided my credit card.

I called back the next day first thing in the morning.

"Have you placed the order," I asked.

"No. Not yet," she said.

"Good! Please, cancel it. I don't like that donor that much."

"Do you have another one in mind?"

"No. I'm hoping for a new one."

"You just call us when you find one a few days in advance. Okay?"

As the day of my cycle approached I got my first faint pink line on the ovulation test and I still didn't have a donor. I wondered again if I should use a known donor. I had considered asking a friend to be the donor but I didn't want to deal with the complications. With a known donor, I had to go to a lawyer and create a contract. Contract and all, a known donor still had paternal rights. If we have to move, my child would be shuffled around two houses not to mention the time spent in court.

Walking into a bar? No way! I wasn't into the bar scene anymore, not since I left Arizona and the thousands of graduate students and young professionals. In Albuquerque I would only find undergraduates at a bar, plus I would have to go by myself. Nah, not me. The Air Force pilots I saw on rare occasions at the base were either too young or both young and married. And again, I would have to deal with courts and custody battles. I didn't want that kind of life and uncertainty for a child. I knew I could provide my child with a stable, loving home by myself.

Once again I went to the drawing board. This time in my search I came up with a profile that had the word **NEW** across the top. I clicked his link.

Hispanic donor, parents born in Mexico. Blue eyes, brown wavy hair. Height: 5 feet, 6 inches. Graduate degree in Sports Medicine, great SAT scores, although not higher than mine. Catholic parents. Loved sushi and writing. His family health history showed no known illness.

That's wonderful! What more could I ask for? Hmm…. Height 5 feet, 6 inches.

I could hear my uncle at the back of my mind saying, "You have to improve our lineage!"

The one time I dated a guy who was 5 feet, 7 inches, it was amazing. He was really cute and I didn't have to wear heels all the time. With all the other ones, dancing strained my neck.

I completed paperwork with his donor number, 11349, and brought it to the clinic.

"How many vials would you like to buy?" the clerk asked me.

"Eight," I answered, and gave her my credit card.

She looked at me with wide eyes.

"I'm not taking risks," I said to her unspoken question. "And I want him off the market."

Back then, I had no idea how ridiculous and impossibly wishful-thinking that idea truly was.

Chapter 9

WHITE DRESS

MY FOURTH ATTEMPT fell on a weekend which meant I didn't have to go to work. I still woke up early because the clinic stopped taking patients at noon on weekends. I knew my routine well and when the nurse left me in the ultrasound room, I changed and sat ready on the examination table. After a few minutes I heard the usual knock on the door.

"Come in," I said.

The nurse followed by the doctor. Not my bald, older doctor, but his young and gorgeous partner. I quickly sat up and covered my knees.

"You're new!" I said, and he laughed. The nurse laughed too.

"No, I'm old. Don't worry," he said as he got closer, "I won't look."

I remembered walking in front of his office and seeing a picture on his desk of him next to a beautiful blond woman and five blond children. I wondered if they had used fertility treatments themselves, but I doubted it. He looked like a donor even more than a doctor.

"You have a polyp!" he said, pointing to the ultrasound monitor. I only saw black and gray shadows.

"What's a polyp?" I asked, wondering if I should know.

"It's a small fibroid," he said. "That's probably why you're not getting pregnant."

"Like a tumor?" I asked.

"Kind of, but polyps are benign and common in many

women," he explained as he completed the test, then he sat on the round stool chair next to me.

I covered myself in the most ladylike fashion I could manage and I turned sideways to face him.

"I've had to travel every time. Maybe that's why I'm not getting pregnant."

"I think it's the polyp," he said.

"So I shouldn't do the insemination today?"

"You can go ahead and do it," he assured me. "Your ovulation looks right. If you don't get pregnant this time, make an appointment with Dr. Jameson to have the polyp removed. It's an outpatient procedure."

I traveled to an academic interview at the University of Texas the week after my fourth procedure. To the previous conferences, I had traveled with co-workers or met up with friends but to the interview I went alone. I truly liked the university and the program. The bioengineering building was brand new. The building had an inner courtyard in the center where students sat and talked, and their voices could be heard all over the building, on the higher floors and corridors. I loved the student atmosphere. I hadn't realized how much I'd missed the energy of having young students around.

My presentation went well and the professors were polite and formal. I felt I had a good chance of getting the job, but something felt odd and I couldn't pinpoint it. The last day of the interview, I waited patiently for the Chair of the department to finish a meeting so he could drive me back to the airport.

I want to go home, I thought while waiting for him. It wasn't only a thought, it was a yearning. *I want to be home right now.*

Where's home? I often wondered.

Home is a Function of Time and Space.

f(H) = S dt

That was the best definition I had come up with. I had attended six schools before college, then my college dorm, four apartments since graduating and two houses after graduate school, so home was what?

Albuquerque? I want to go back to Albuquerque?

After graduate school, I wanted to go where I could see the ocean. Somewhere like San Diego or Florida. I had taken a detour before working at The Labs and spent six months working as a researcher in Tampa. I had to cross a long bridge to get to Largo to get to work every morning. I loved Florida so much that after six months it was difficult to have to pack and leave. When I moved to Albuquerque everything looked brown, my least favorite color. In Florida and Puerto Rico the predominant colors were blue and green, blue like the ocean and green like the trees. In Arizona, the mountains looked red, my favorite color.

In Albuquerque, I decided to buy rather than rent, my first home.

"You better make it a mobile home," my cousins joked.

Buying a house kept the move interesting and exciting. When I first drove to it with my real estate agent, we turned left on a street light that had Costco on one corner and a large park and recreational center on the other side. The houses were behind Costco. Although most houses I had seen in Albuquerque were Pueblo-style with flat roofs, the houses in my new neighborhood had gable roofs with dormer windows, all in tiles of varying colors, from cream and terracotta to maroon. The house walls were painted in light pastel colors.

"They look like Barbie houses!" I exclaimed as soon as I saw them.

To enter the neighborhood we had to get access through

massive black gates. My house was in a cul-de-sac, and from the road I could tell the back windows had a view of the park we had passed next to Costco.

My real estate agent pointed to the mailboxes across the street. Behind the mailboxes, sat a small park with perfectly manicured golf-green grass and a small playground in the center.

"It's perfect," I said and I didn't want to consider any other houses.

Moving to Texas for this academi job, though, meant having to learn new roads, having to find a new house, a new supermarket, a new church.

I'm tired of this gypsy life, I thought as I waited and waited for the Chair to finish his meeting.

I will also have to wait for tenure.

Getting pregnant during my first year as a professor, while setting up a lab and applying to grants, was out of the question. If I wanted tenure, I would have to wait a few more years to try to get pregnant.

I thought about a discussion panel at one of the conferences I had attended recently. The discussion was about the lack of women in engineering professions, including academic and high management positions. The conclusion of the seminar was that gender discrimination played a huge role, but so did the lack of support for professional women during their child-bearing years. Women who chose to have children were seen as non-competitive in their professions. Although a high percentage of women graduated with a degree in engineering, by their late 20's they had disappeared from the profession. The discussion was attended by an executive from the NIH, the National Institute of Health.

"What do women need to stay active in their careers," he asked the panel. Various suggestions were offered, including child-care at or near work.

It must have been the anger in my eyes and my clenched teeth that made the NIH professional seek me out afterwards to ask me my thoughts on the subject.

"Why do I have to choose?" I asked. "As a girl I was given dolls to play with, and I was told I could be anything I wanted. Why do I have to choose between my career and being a mother? Why after coming this far, I have to give up one of my dreams?"

He listened and nodded. He didn't come up with a solution fast enough.

Back at the University of Texas, I held my carry-on close to my chest and I leaned my head on the handle. When the Chair walked out of his office he laughed at me.

"You look bored," he said and I sat up straight.

The Chair drove me to the airport a few hours before my flight. Instead of checking-in right away, I took a taxi to the nearest mall. My brother's birthday was the next day and I still had to buy him a present.

The mall was small and boring but it had a Macy's. I found a Nautica shirt and tie he would like, now that he had started to date a girl from our new neighborhood. A look at my watch told me I still had plenty of time before my flight so I went in search of a Hallmark store to get my brother a card. I was hoping to find a *Happy Birthday Uncle* card, to make the announcement to my brother at the same time, if I ended up with a positive result. Luckily I found a Hallmark close to Macy's. I went in and chose a card. When I walked out of Hallmark, I came face to face with a Bridal shop. I stared at a beautiful white dress on the window display. I looked at it for as long as I dared, afraid of being noticed. I wanted to walk in, but I didn't. I wanted to try on the dress.

I would look great in an off-the-shoulder dress, I thought. I couldn't afford to be late, so I walked out of the mall and back to the taxi.

My brother and Kim, his new girlfriend, picked me up at the airport in Albuquerque. Once home, my brother took my suitcase upstairs. I wanted to show Kim the present I had gotten for my brother, so I opened my carry-on and as soon as I took out the unwrapped box, another box was plainly visible: the box of pregnancy tests. I tried to close the bag quickly, but I wasn't quick enough. Kim had seen what it was.

"I forgot that was there," I said.

She gave me an understanding look. "Insemination?"

"Yes," I nodded. "I don't talk about it because my brother doesn't want to hear about it."

"He's being silly," she said shaking her head. "Any news?"

"I won't know for another few days."

A few days later, I made an appointment to get the darn poly removed.

Chapter 10

DEFINITELY/MAYBE

I WAS INSTRUCTED to take an antibiotic and acetaminophen, not ibuprofen, before the polyp removal since the polyp was going to be cut off and scraped from the wall of my uterus. Dr. Jameson, my bald doctor, performed the procedure. He kept me informed of his observations.

"I see the polyp, but I don't think I will be able to remove it now."

"Why not?"

"It's not easy to reach. It's incrusted into the wall of your uterus. Even if I scrape, it won't come out. It's too big."

"How big?" I asked. I hadn't asked the other doctor details about my polyp, but I thought it was something the size of a grape seed. Anything bigger sounded dangerous.

Dr. Jameson formed a circle with his thumb and index finger. "About the size of a golf ball."

"What?" I asked. "That's huge!"

"It's a normal size for a polyp," he assured me. "But I won't be able to remove it in the clinic. It has to be by surgery."

"Surgery?" I suddenly felt dizzy. A golf ball was not a tiny polyp, it was a real big tumor. A tumor that needed an invasive surgery to be removed. I suddenly regretted having stared at the white dress on the window display at the store. I didn't want to wear a white dress. I wanted to be a mother and I suddenly felt my chances slipping away.

Surgery!

I left the clinic in a state of shock and once outside the hospital I knew my self-control was slipping away, so I crossed the street to the parking in a hurry and locked myself in my car. Once inside, I covered my mouth with my hand and cried.

I called my boss and told him I needed the rest of the day off. I went home instead to cry alone. I knew at some point I needed to call my mother and tell her the news. My mother, who had her uterus removed at the age of 26, right after giving birth to my brother because of a fibroid. My mother wasn't the only one in my family. My second cousin, who went to kindergarten with me had a fibroid removed. Hers wasn't just any fibroid, it was cancer. She had to have a hysterectomy and chemotherapy and was never able to have children of her own.

It was too much for me. I couldn't call anyone in the state I was in. I had to calm myself down, so I grabbed my purse and went out to see a movie.

I chose a movie that had nothing to do with cancer or fibroids. The title of the movie was *Definitely, Maybe*, a romantic comedy.

Except the movie was about a guy who had a great friend by his side but he didn't choose her. He married someone else and had a child and ten years later he came back and wanted to be with her.

Ten years later? Whatever for! And the tears started again.

I didn't hear from Hubbell for about ten years when he suddenly appeared on *Linked In*. I got a notification that he had looked at my page, not once but a few times. I ignored him at first but then he sent an invitation to connect. I didn't want him in my professional life and I definitely didn't want him in my private life, so I pressed *Ignore* and managed to do that for about a year. Ten years before his last words to me had not only hurt me, they had offended me. Somedays I dreamed of throwing his words back at him and rubbing them all over his face.

I wanted to shout at him. "No, I can't accept your *Friend Request* because you don't deserve to be my friend!"

After a while, instead of accepting the Linked In connection I send him a message.

"If you have something to say to me just send me an email," and I gave him my email address, not the email from ASU, but the one I had gotten after he was out of my life. Within a day I received an email from him.

> Hi Lania-
>
> Glad to hear from you...it's been a long time.... I hope you're doing well. I'm in a bit of a quandary, a bifurcation at the least....
>
> But, how are you? Family? Work? Life?
>
> Hope you're doing well,
> H.

The movie *Definitely Maybe* didn't help keep the fibroid away from my mind or the tears from my eyes. As I walked out of the theater, I tried to hide my face, especially since no one else seemed to be crying. I still didn't feel ready to call my mother. I needed to go somewhere else. I decided to stop at a Native American jewelry store.

After I graduated from ASU and moved to Florida, my boss there had asked me if I had bought any Indian jewelry.

"No," I had to answer. "I was a student."

Now I had a salary and no dependents. The store had plenty of options but I found myself staring at their hand-crafted exclusive collection. The store owner walked over and asked if I wanted a closer look at any of the pieces. I debated between a coral set, which I would wear often because it was my favorite color or a turquoise set on heavy silver which looked like jewelry for Tribal Royalty. I pointed to the turquoise necklace and tried it on. I loved it.

"Can I see the matching earrings and bracelet?" I asked. The silver bracelet felt cool and heavier than any jewelry I had ever worn. After rubbing the earring in isopropanol, they let me try them too. The earrings looked smaller but also heavier than the ones I usually wore. They pulled my earlobe down a bit, but they were the only ones that looked perfect with the necklace. The necklace was also made of solid silver, had the marks of the stone in which it was set and hand-crafted Indian designs. It fell in a "V" shape below my neck and ended with an oval turquoise the same color as the earrings. All three pieces looked beautiful together and I wasn't willing to take them off.

"I want them," I said to the lady. Each one of the three pieces had a price tag attached but I didn't focus on the price. I was determined to have them.

The store owner marked the numbers on the cash register and informed me of the total cost, then she added their store discount and tax. I took my debit card out of my purse and handed it to her.

After leaving the store, I knew I was ready to call my mother. Mainly because I felt more in shock at the $800 purchase than about the surgery.

"My doctor said I have a fibroid the size of a golf ball and he wasn't able to remove it in the clinic so I need surgery," I said to my dad since he was the one to answer the phone.

"Wow," he said. He was quiet for a few seconds, then we continued talking about something else.

That was good practice, I thought.

Then it was my mother's turn. I told her about the stupid movie I had just seen. We then talked about my brother's relationship with his new girlfriend.

"What was that you told your father?" my mother asked.

"I had a doctor's appointment today," I said. "He said the polyp was a bit bigger and he couldn't remove it in his office."

"How big?" my mother asked.

"He said about the size of a gold ball."

"A golf ball? That's gigantic! My God. What is he going to do?"

I took a deep breath and changed my cell phone, which already felt hot, to my other ear. "He said it has to be done through surgery."

I heard my mother gasp. "I had a fibroid after your brother was born," she said. "And they removed my uterus and everything else."

We were both silent for a while and I tried not to cry, to not make things worse.

"I'll be there tomorrow. I have to talk to your doctor."

"Oh, no! No, no!" I tried to dissuade her, but she dug her heels until I gave in and asked for a special consult with my Dr. Jameson.

Jameson met us in front of his office and welcomed us in. After introductions and pleasantries we sat down, holding our purses on our laps. While the doctor cleared his throat I reached into my purse for my silver "thinking pen" which I always carried with me for moments like this. My mother jumped right into her questions.

"Hers is a large tumor," she stated.

His face gesture indicated he didn't think of it as large. "It is about the size of your fist," he said, showing us *his* closed fist.

My mother's eyes widened. "One like that forced me to have a hysterectomy when I was 26 years old, right after giving birth to my son."

Dr. Jameson nodded. "Studies show fibroids are more common on African Americans and Latino women."

My mother nodded as well. "What are the chances it could be malignant?"

This time Dr. Jameson shook his head. "Most fibroids are not malignant, but we can do a biopsy to confirm that's the case, if there's suspicion."

"Will she have to get chemo?" she asked.

"I doubt it," he answered.

"What are the chances the size could be reduced with medication?" my mother asked, providing the names of specific medications off the top of her head.

He shook his head and answered something along the lines of, "That medication reduces the size of the tumor but then the tumor starts to grow again."

My mother slowly nodded. She took a sideway look at me, a look that changed from me being the patient in question to being her little girl. She faced him again.

"What are the chances of hysterectomy?"

He quickly shook his head. "In this clinic we treat fertility. That means we do everything in our power to protect the uterus. The only way we would need to remove the uterus is in case of excessive bleeding, which could jeopardize her life during surgery."

My mother's eyes grew big and she sat further back against her seat. "And after surgery?"

He nodded this time. "I recommend three months of recovery before she goes back into fertility treatments."

They both turned to me. My back remained straight during their conversation and the cat had my tongue. "Can I try IVF before deciding if I want surgery?"

Dr. Jameson shook his dead. "I would not recommend that. IVF is too expensive and difficult. With a fibroid like yours, the chance of a miscarriage increases."

I grew quiet again. There was nothing I feared more than a miscarriage, not even the surgery. "The surgery will take a while to get scheduled. Can I complete IVF paperwork at the same time?"

He nodded. "For three months after the surgery."

I nodded in agreement. "And can I continue with IUI's until the time of surgery?"

He nodded and I breathed a sigh of relief.

Chapter 11

TELL HIM

January 2000

AFTER THE HOLIDAYS of our FIRST YEAR IN GRAD SCHOOL, Hubbell and I casually met at the stairs of the Engineering building. He walked downstairs while I walked up.

"Hey!" His usual greeting came out sounding happy to see me.

"Hey," I smiled back and my eyes hugged him. I walked up a few more steps, to be eye level with him and he followed me with his gaze.

"How was your break?" His hands held on to his camouflage sling bag. My fingers rested on the straps of my red backpack.

"Great," I said beaming. "I went to the beach with my brother for Christmas! How about you?"

He snorted. "I went ice finishing by myself."

"Cool! Did you have to make a whole in the ice? How do you do that?"

"We have a special device that cuts it."

"I'd love to try it!"

"No, you wouldn't," he snorted. "You'd freeze your butt off. You'd have to sit in the car for hours to try and keep warm while you wait for a catch."

"Yikes," I had to re-think that one. What a contrast to the warm non-insulated and dusty staircase area. "How's Gini?" I asked, guessing he had spent time with his best friend.

"She's all right," he shrugged.,

"And your sister? Any kids yet?"

"No," he snorted more loudly. "She's only been married a couple of years."

I climbed up a few more steps, pretending to be moving towards my destination to get my semester classes. "That's enough time," I said. "Most of my friends have children soon after marriage. Like six months."

He laughed. "They wanna wait," he said shrugging. "Hey, I just heard the guys are having a Back to School party. You going?"

"I haven't heard about it yet."

"Check your email."

A few more glances later, I pretended it was time to go get my new class schedule.

"See you!" he said. I dragged myself away.

It was karaoke night at the guys house. They had their usual keg, a couple boxes of wine and a brand new foosball table in the center of what should have been their dining room. Hubbell was engrossed in a foosball match with a guy I hadn't met. I grabbed a red plastic cup and headed for the keg, deciding for bad beer over bad wine. That's when I saw them, the Three Amigas: the blond, the bleached, and the miniskirt. My blood froze. I looked at Hubbell feeling betrayed as he looked up from his game to gage my reaction. His game finished soon after and he walked over to the counter and settled next to me.

"Hey," he said.

"Hi," I said without looking at him. "What are they doing here?" I didn't have to point at the trio, he knew what I meant.

"Don't you know?" he asked. "Ron's been dating the one on the left. They got engaged over the break."

"Uh," I swallowed a gulp of warm, bitter beer. "Guess they're going to be around, then."

"Guess so," he said. He switched the conversation to the older graduate student he had been playing with.

"His wife cheated on him. It's so unfair because he's a really nice guy. She's a total bitch."

We talked until the guys called Hubbell to help get the karaoke set up and started.

JW, the cutest one of the guys, made an attempt at singing but he kept breaking into laughter. Ron's new fiancé took the microphone from him and changed the song to Faith Hill's "This Kiss" and the other two amigas joined her.

"It's centrifugal motion…" they sang in unison.

I bet they don't know what centrifugal motion is, I thought. They had decent voices, which meant I would stay the hell away from the karaoke all night, even though I had walked in singing "Brown Eyed Girl," the song playing on the radio when I walked into the house.

The nice guy who had been cheated on, saw that I was alone and sat next to me. He introduced himself and for lack of better company I stayed talking to him. After the amigas got tired of singing, Hubbell grabbed the microphone to sing "It's Been a While."

"You better not dedicate that song to me," I said to him one night at my place. I thought it was a creepy song, but he liked it.

Hubbell had a deep husky voice. Not bad but not great either.

The nice guy next to me asked me something and I nodded absently, so he grabbed my empty cup and re-filled it with beer from a new fresh keg.

Hubbell's song ended and he walked into the kitchen as the nice guy handed me the fresh cup of beer.

It happened quickly. Miniskirt broke from her trio and walked over to Hubbell.

"We are going to *Federico's*, would you like to come?"

Hubbell looked at me from across the kitchen and I stared back at him. I shook my head slowly so no one else would see except him. Hubbell said something to the girl and she left. Hubbell didn't look at me on his way to the main room. He sat fuming on the worn black leather sofa.

I felt bad for Hubbell but relieved for myself. When I turned back to Nice Guy, I realized he was looking at me.

"What was that?" he asked pointing his chin toward the black leather sofa.

I took a deep breath and bit my nails. "I like him," I said.

Nice guy nodded. "Have you told him?" his tone changed to older-brotherly.

"Nope," I admitted.

"Tell him," he said. He explained all the reasons why a guy would not easily tell a girl that he liked her.

Tell him, my brain echoed. This advice was too familiar, history repeating itself no matter how much I tried to escape.

"Tell him you love him," my mother had advised years before in a different situation, with a different best friend. I took her advice and told him, but it changed nothing.

"Go," the nice guy urged and I looked at the gloomy Hubbell again.

I smiled at Nice Guy and walked over to the leather sofa.

I sat next to Hubbell and tried to look at him but he wouldn't look up.

"I'm sorry," I offered honestly.

"You had no right," he said, sounding pissed. "They were being nice and they were only going to the drive-through."

Ouch. "I know. I think I better explain." I tried to take a deep breath, but instead I held it in. "I'm crazy about you, Hubbell."

He smiled.

Silence.

Hubbell's best friend, the smartest one of the three housemates, startled us. I felt over-conscious of my nearness to Hubbell, so I scooted some distance away. I wanted a chance to talk to him again, but the chance never came that night. Or the next day. Or during the week in class.

I asked him on Friday as we worked on a project for our Advance Statistics class and sharing information over messenger.

"Any thoughts about what you're going to do?"

"About the conclusion?"

"No the project, silly. About your mid-life crisis."

"Oh," he said, as if that was the furthest thing in his mind. "My ex wants to get back together."

"Really? I didn't know."

"Yeah."

"How nice," I said sarcastically. "A new variable to the equation! What conclusion, if any, have you reached?"

"Don't know." I knew he was shrugging at the other end and cracking his neck.

My hands jumped away from the keyboard and formed into fists. "At least tell me what you think about me," I wrote.

"You and I seem to have a massive difference in opinions."

Really? I thought. "About religion?"

"Yeah, about that too. Who's next?" he asked.

That's it? That's all you have to say about me? "What will you do about *Miniskirt*?"

"She's okay, but I fear you won't talk to me again if I date her."

"I won't," I wrote back. "I can't stand her."

"Figured. I don't know why you have to be like that."

"Let me remind you. Remember the time we all went to that restaurant and the Three Amigas asked if I was the waitress?"

"That wasn't her. That was Blond, and I admit, Blond is not the sharpest tool in the shed."

"They're all the same, Hubbell."

"Whatever," he said. "What else you wanna know?"

"Does that mean you're getting back with your ex?" I asked.

"...." he wrote, which was our code for "Thinking about it."

I wanted to ask so much more. Actually, no, I wanted him to say so much more but he didn't. *Why couldn't he see we were great together? So, his family was from Montana and mine from Puerto Rico. So what? We both come from middle class families. I'm a Catholic and so is his mother. We are studying the same career at the same university, and everyone knows we are inseparable.*

Was that not good enough for him? Or was I not good enough for him?

We finished the project. I printed mine and shoved it into my backpack.

Later that day, my roommate treated me to a chocolate shopping spree. Back home, we sat across our Kmart dining table drinking Hard Lemonade and eating slices of our triple chocolate cake when our friend, Maria, called.

My roommate and I, on occasions, hung out with a small group of Puerto Ricans, most of them from the Architecture Department. They had a favorite restaurant bar and I liked the feeling of the familiar. I forked around the half-eaten piece of cake and thought of an excuse to not go.

"Go!" I saw my roommate mouth.

I pointed at her, "You go!" I mouthed back.

She shook her head in horror, and I knew she had burned bridges with our fellow countrymen, and women.

What would I have to lose? I sighed and told Maria I would be there.

It was another hot day in Arizona so I decided to wear my favorite red bare-back top. Red was my color, the one I looked best in and the one I chose for extra confidence. The shirt matched my khaki capris, the only problem was that the chocolate calories had not done their damage yet and over my first year in graduate school I had lost weight.

"You look like you dug into your mother's closet," my roommate said and handed me a pair of black capris. They fit like a glove. I sprayed on my favorite perfume, grabbed my purse and slipped my feet into my 3-inch platform sandals.

When I arrived at the bar, Maria wasn't there yet but even through the dim lights, I immediately spotted the two new students Maria had introduced to the group at a previous party. I squeezed through to their table. They seemed happy to see me and were full of compliments. Maria arrived soon after with my roommate's ex-fling. She greeted me with an air kiss and hug, and asked me to sit next to her at the bar. Her friend stayed behind, talking to the two new guys. Maria and I both ordered Coronas and she asked how I was doing. I told her about Hubbell and my frustration with my miniskirt-archenemy.

Half way through my beer Maria finished hers and on-cue, *ex-fling* stood next to her and ordered her a new one. She tried hard to pretend his proximity wasn't affecting her but I could tell she had stopped listening to me. The two new guys came over to my side and through the blaring sound of *Mambo Number 5,* asked if I wanted another beer. I pushed my warm beer aside and nodded.

I turned back to Maria. "So what do you think I should do?" I asked her.

"Huh?" she turned from ex-*fling* back to me but I could tell I had lost her.

The new guys came back with my beer and stayed talking to me most of the night. One of them in particular stood closer to my chair, as if claiming me. He played with my hair and at one point placed his arm around my shoulders. My melancholy slipped away as I delighted in his attention.

This was what Puerto Rican guys were like. Why couldn't Hubbell be more like this? I wondered.

He wasn't particularly my type, a bit too angular, while I preferred smooth muscled men, but he was good looking. Several years later, the werewolf from The Twilight Saga would remind me of him, so I nicknamed him Jacob.

Some beers later, Jacob grabbed the string that crisscrossed across my back and kept my shirt tied. "What happens if I pull this?" he asked playfully.

"You can try," I replied with a flirty smile, "but I plan for idiots like you and knot it twice."

"Ugh, burnt!" his friend chuckled and Jacob dropped the string and nodded, accepting defeat.

When I had enough beers, I asked Jacob if he would walk me to my car. I usually asked someone to walk with me for safety, and that someone was usually Hubbell.

Jacob not only walked with me, he also held my hand the entire way. When I was close to my door, I turned to say goodbye but he backed me up against my car and placed both hands against it, locking me in. He looked at me, asking, and my training of two summers before kicked in.

The summer I finished my undergrad, I traveled to Paris with the French Club. Our chaperone, a gay professor, taught my friends and I a valuable lesson.

"Stay safe, but don't deny a kiss to a poor dog!"

I looked into Jacob's eyes, then to his full lips. Would they feel as warm as they looked? I closed the gap between us and let him kiss me. His arms moved from my car to my lower back until he happened upon the strap again.

"Come with me to my apartment," he said, gasping between kisses. "I want to show you my flag."

"Flag?" my eyebrows raised.

"I decorated a wall with our country flag," he explained.

"Oh!" I thought. "Okay."

A question came to my mind as we sat in my car. "Are you with anyone else," I wanted to know before we headed anywhere.

"No," he assured me. "I mean, no girlfriend or anything like that."

"Good," I said and I turned the ignition.

I went with him to his apartment and spent the night with him. He was nice enough to walk me to my car right before dawn.

"Will I see you again?" he asked, letting go of my hand.

"I don't know," I shrugged. "If I see you, I see you and if not, that's fine too." After all, I wasn't impressed by his flag or his... patriotism.

"Ha!" he laughed, looking up at the stars. "I feel used."

I laughed, too.

Instead of accepting my decision, he insisted on watching a movie together the next weekend and the next, until I started thinking we had something more and I ventured out to visit him in his apartment. Suddenly he wasn't all that happy to see me. We sat down on the floor of the hallway in front of his closed apartment door.

"What's wrong?" I asked.

He shook his head. "It's my friends. My roommate."

"Your roommate?"

"I mean, my roommate and the other architects. We're all from the same university back home. They know each other and you know how news travels." He nervously moved his hands as he spoke.

"Really?" I wondered. "Why do you care what they say."

He snorted out, exasperated. "I don't want to be seen with you."

"Oh!" It took a millisecond for my temper to flare. My hands flew to my waist. "I'm not the kind of girl anyone should be ashamed of!"

"It's not you," he tried to back away. "There's this girl back home, and the other architects know her."

"And you say that now? Wasn't that the first fucking thing I asked you?" It should have been so obvious, I fumed. *This was exactly what Puerto Rican guys were like.*

He looked at me with sad pound dog eyes. I wasn't having it.

"This ends now," I told him. "Whatever this was or wasn't," I clarified, "it's over right now."

As I explained to my roommate the next morning, I cried a tear for the fool I had been. A single one. He wasn't worth more.

All my life I have been proud of how I acted. I had fun, then I ended it, swiftly and painlessly. I wasn't so proud of what I did next.

I had been in high spirits the last couple of weeks. The whole thing with Jacob had heightened my confidence. The College of Engineering had a showcase of their different departments for all of ASU. They had tents and tables set up for each department. Our Chair had asked us, his group of favorite students, to participate. Hubbell and I, along with the housemates and a couple other classmates, took turns at our booth. Hubbell and one of the guys sat on chairs but I felt too exuberant to sit still, so I lounged on the table. Our classmate's pretty girlfriend joined me. At noon Hubbell said he was hungry and asked me if I wanted to get something to eat with him.

We walked over to the Memorial Union, side by side. We chatted easily the entire way there.

"Guess what?" I said when we sat down with our food.

"What?" he asked with his mouth full.

"I met someone," I told him.

"Really!" he asked, not too surprised, and took another bite. "Have you seen him more than once?"

"A few times," I admitted. "We spent some nights together."

Hubbell stopped chewing and swallowed hard. "Hm," he said, and looked away from me.

"We had sex," I said.

He put his unfinished hamburger down on the tray. "Why are you telling me this?" He sounded annoyed.

To get a reaction from you. To make you jealous, like you've been making me feel! "Because you're my friend. Who else would I tell?"

He took a couple more big bites, then dumped his tray. On our way back he stalked in front of me as I tried hard to catch up. I had the horrible feeling I had made a huge mistake.

Chapter 12

SECOND OPINION

THE WORST PART about surgery wasn't the physical pain, it was the stab to my pride. I consulted with my twin-look-alike friend from grade school, my renegade soulmate from our high school years, who had become a surgeon while I attended grad school.

"Yari, is it really necessary?"

"Of course it is," she answered casually. "You need to have it removed."

"Uh, Yari, it's in my uterus, not a splinter on my foot!"

I made an appointment with my hippie OB, the one who had referred me to Dr. Jameson.

"Is it really, really necessary?"

"That's probably why you're not getting pregnant," she said. "There's no implantation on the fibroid tissue."

I reluctantly signed the papers for surgery at the fertility doctor, begged him not to remove my uterus under any circumstance and attended the hospital pre-admission interview.

The day before surgery, I had to start fasting at midnight. My family took me to a Tepan restaurant for dinner. My brother and father tried to keep the mood light by making casual jokes but I wasn't in the mood. My mother's phone rang and she went outside to answer it. She returned smiling.

"It was Abuela. She wanted to know what we were doing."

"The Last Supper," I muttered dryly.

That night, I could not sleep. I turned and turned in bed.

My body was in a constant state of utter awareness and my brain would not stop the annoying thinking.

I needed to call someone, but who? It was the middle of the work week. I had waited too late, now all my Arizona friends were sleeping.

Who lives at a later time zone?

Hubbell?

No!

Even if I could trace him down at this hour, I still didn't want anything to do with him.

Then who? And it hit me.

Sweet Thing! He lived in California.

Wondering if he still had the same phone number, I looked up his name on my phone and called.

Chapter 13

THE ONE WHO COULD HAVE BEEN

"HEEYYYY....!" SWEET THING, Allen, said on the other end and I breathed a sigh of relief at the familiar sweetness of his voice.

Years ago, when my cousins and I started dating, my youngest aunt said to us,

"Marry someone who will have no problem hanging out in Abuela's backyard, with the chicken walking around and pooping everywhere."

I knew she meant this advice primarily for me, the proudest, the most ambitious, the fanciest, but her words didn't take me by surprise. I saw truth and logic in them. We all loved hanging out at Abuela's house, backyard, front yard, balcony, terrace, rooms and kitchen. The house was small by current standards, but it comfortably fit all six of her children with their spouses, all of her grandchildren and great-grandchildren. Most family gatherings consisted of at least 50 people. Abuela's home was home to all of us.

Slowly, my cousins started bringing home only those candidates that would sit comfortably around chicken poop and that's how we knew they were keepers. They chose well. They fit in with our family seamlessly.

Except for me. I never brought anyone to Abuela's house. Certainly not Hubbell, who was too xenophobic to travel to Puerto Rico, let alone feel comfortable sitting around people who didn't speak his language.

Then there was Allen.

I met Allen the summer between my first and second year of grad school. The Chair of Bioengineering hosted an awards dinner at his house and Adam and I were introduced as the new leaders of the professional clubs for the upcoming year. I would be leading the graduate club and Allen the undergraduate one. Allen and I were officially introduced by the Chair, we shook hands and sat next to each other. His self-confidence was obvious when he initiated a conversation with me that lasted through the night. I noticed how cute he was, with his auburn hair, square jaw, greenish-blue eyes and cleft chin. His white polo shirt and jeans added the final touch to his preppy look.

"Go hit on freshman girls!" I told him after a long stare between us.

He smiled but lowered his gaze and I immediately regretted inflicting that low blow. Still, that didn't deter Allen. Just the opposite. Every time I called Allen, he rushed there. A few months into the school year he came to me and told me he wanted to spend the summer in a country where he could practice his Spanish. I called my parents and asked if Allen could spend the summer with them, and that's what he did.

I went home for a week that summer, but before I got there I learned Allen had bought a bicycle so he could ride to Abuela's house.

"Bendicion, Abuela," he would tell her, like all of us did.

"Hola hijo, como estas?"

"Muy bien."

"Quieres cafe?"

"Por supuesto!" Allen would say, which always made Abuela laugh, but she would prepare a fresh pot of coffee especially for him and they would sit on the balcony, talking and waving at neighbors passing by.

I traveled to my hometown for a week that summer, to attend my brother's college graduation. After the formal event and the celebration at home, it was nice to spend the rest of the week touring the Island with Allen. We went to Ponce with my younger cousin, who was as close to Allen in age as he was to me. She flirted with him the same way she flirted with every boy around her. I wondered if she and Allen would be a good fit, but it didn't matter much. We were being young and having fun. I pointed Allen to places of interest and took pictures of him in front of those places. Allen took pictures of my cousin and I posing together.

We drove to Old San Juan and visited El Morro, the Spanish fort built for the defense of the Island from invading countries. During different periods of time, countries like France, Italy, Poland, Spain, of course, and eventually the United States all claimed ownership of Puerto Rico. Combine that with the Natives and African slaves, and the result was a diverse and rich population and culture.

Inside El Morro, I took a picture of Allen at La Garita, a watch window famously known for soldiers disappearing. Every window led to a beautiful view of the Atlantic Ocean.

"Isn't it beautiful?" I asked him often.

He nodded in agreement. "It has its share of beauty."

On my weekend before flying back to ASU, Allen and I went with my cousin, her husband, my brother and his girlfriend to the Fluorescent Bay at La Parguera. We had to wait for a moonless night to get the best view of the fluorescent microorganisms that gave the ocean waters its luminescence. We paid for a boat tour. As the boat drifted away from the city lights, under the pitch black sky a million stars could be seen reflecting on the water below.

"Is that part of the fluorescence?" Allen asked.

"No, it's more subtle and at the same time more amazing. Just wait for it."

The boat stopped in the middle of nowhere and the driver killed the engine. He pointed to the area where the fluorescence should be seen. We couldn't really see much and I felt deflated. I knew pollution was affecting the fluorescent waters. Then one of the tour guides took off his shirt and dove into the water, creating a splash of fluorescence that left us Ooh-ing and Aww-ing.

Then like a merman, he resurfaced from the water and his entire body shone with millions of sparkles.

"Oh!" Allen whispered. "It's sooo…." but he couldn't find words to describe it.

The tour guide-merman swam around the boat for everyone to see.

"It's perfect for…" Allen started but didn't complete the sentence.

"Skinny dipping," I finished for him.

"Hey!" he said.

I laughed. "Wasn't that what you had in mind?"

I couldn't tell, but I think he blushed. Allen blushed easily. Not me. I wanted really bad to undress and jump into the water, even without a swimsuit. If it had been just me and Allen, nothing would have stopped me, but the boat was full of people.

Seeing their customers were more than satisfied with the experience, the boat's engine started again and we headed back to the pier. Now that our curiosity of the fluorescence had been satisfied, the passengers sat relaxed and quiet. The boat was large enough for us to walk around and I wanted to enjoy every minute of my last weekend on my Island of Enchantment. I went to the side of the boat and held onto the rail as the boat sped forward. The waves made the boat pop up and down. I lowered my head towards the water to take in the cool moist air and laughed when the fiercest jolt sprayed my face with salt water. I could smell and taste the saltiness on my skin.

I became aware of someone approaching and didn't have to turn to know it was Allen. He got closer until his elbow graced my arm.

Is he looking out into the sea, enjoying the experience or is he looking at me? I wanted to turn to figure it out but at the same time I felt the dread of knowing he wasn't looking out to sea. He was very close and I knew what would happen if I looked at him. I knew what I would do.

People ask me, "What is your biggest regret in life?"

"Nothing," I answer. "I don't do things I could regret, so I never have to regret the things I do."

In truth, it is not the things I do. It's the things I don't do.

Why not kiss him? I asked myself.

It wasn't lack of courage. It was everything happening that summer at ASU.

"Heyyy...!" Allen answered my call the night before my surgery, and I breathed a sigh of relief upon hearing his friendly voice.

"Sweet Thing!"

"What a surprise! Where in the world are you?"

I sat up in bed. "I'm still in Albuquerque."

"What's going on?" he asked.

"I'm having surgery tomorrow," I blurted out.

"Ah," he said. "You couldn't sleep. You're over-worrying about it."

"How do you know?" I wondered. Had he been talking with my mom?

"I've had knee surgery, so I know how it feels."

"Oh," I sighed in relief.

We talked about the reason for my surgery but I didn't tell him about the other reason, the main one. I wasn't ready for any of my friends to know. I still felt uncertain and vulnerable as to whether it would work or not.

We talked for a long while.

"Why are you afraid?" he asked. "It's not like you."

"I'm afraid something might go wrong, and you know, not being able to have children. Like later on."

"That makes sense," he replied.

He then told me about his experience with surgery and assured me it would all turn out okay. I believed him. It was so meant to be that I would call the one person who would understand me best.

I once believed Allen and I were meant to be.

Then there was that bit of a pause, that lapse of time in which our main topic of conversation was over and we didn't know what to say next. I didn't want to ask the question in my mind and I didn't want to hang up even though my flip phone already felt hot against my ear. I kept having to switch it between my left and right ears.

"I should probably hang up," I finally said after that short endless silence. "I don't want your wife to get mad."

"Nah, it's okay," he replied and sighed while I waited, holding my breath and mad at myself. "I didn't get married."

What? I thought. Had I heard him right?

"We broke the engagement," he said, confirming my unspoken question.

The summer Allen stayed in Puerto Rico was amazing.

"Is he the one?" Abuela asked me.

I shrugged. "He's too young, Abuela."

"Oh, a few years here or there don't matter much."

I knew she was right. In the overall scheme of things, it didn't really matter.

On my last evening in town we drove to the mall to run an errand for my mother. As we crossed the parking lot he noticed people staring at him. Puerto Ricans come in every color under the rainbow, even within the same family, but Allen's extra pale skin and reddish hair drew attention to him. It wasn't only the reflection of his skin under every type of lighting, it was also his taller and broader frame. Not to mention the way he dressed.

"Are you ashamed to be seen with me?" he asked, catching me off-guard and I chuckled as I looked down at the socks he wore with sandals.

"Of course not!" I assured him. To prove my point, I crossed my arm with his. "Are you ashamed to be seen with me when we're in Arizona?"

"No," he said firmly.

I knew he meant it. It would not have occurred to him.

Way too soon that summer, I returned to Arizona, to Sparky and to Hubbell.

Things had not started well that summer with Hubbell. Before the semester ended we had traveled to a Biomedical conference in Seattle, where his ex-girlfriend officially lost the title of *ex*. Things had worked out so well during the conference they decided to move in together as soon as she graduated.

Also that summer one of the professors announced he had been given a position at a different university. He decided to move his research lab, along with his graduate students, which included all of the house-mates.

The start of the summer carried a simmering air of melancholy, especially for Hubbell. He felt an urgency to enjoy every second left of his time with the guys who had been our best friends. They went out every night to sports bars. After a few drinks, Hubbell deemed it necessary to avoid an additional left turn while still buzzed.

"Can I have some water?" He always asked for water when he came to see me. Some nights I would have the cup ready for him.

"How's the level of blood in your alcoholic veins?"

We were not required to take classes over the summer. Instead, we worked on our research, to get as much done before classes started again. Hubbell got to his lab around 10am. I rarely made it to mine until closer to noon. I had to pass his lab on the way to mine. I always walked pretending not to look into his lab. The idea was to let him see me.

Some labs had multiple graduate students working in them,

but in mine it was usually just me. Everyone left their lab doors open. Interruptions from work were more than welcome. I also left my door open and within minutes Hubbell walked in.

"What up?"

"I'm still setting up."

He walked closer to my bench. "What are you working with today?"

"I'm coating paramagnetic particles with dendrimers." I showed him the contents of my 10mL flask.

"A dark solution? How do you know there's anything there?"

To show him, I placed a rare earth magnet underneath the flask. Immediately the substances divided. The top liquid became clear while the paramagnetic particles, or what he called the dark solution, gathered to the bottom of the flask. I removed the magnet and stirred the flask and the particles dispersed in solution again.

"Cool! Looks more interesting than my project."

I thought so, but I didn't tell him. I felt proud of his work with ultrasound too.

"Wanna go to lunch in a bit?"

"Yeah, let me start the reaction and then I can go."

One weekend, I hurt my ankle while jet skiing with friends. He saw me limping in front of his lab door and asked me what happened.

"It's not as bad as your football injury," I assured him. His ankle had turned black, purple and blue. I walked inside the lab and sat on a chair next to his desk.

"Let me take a look," he said.

"You won't see anything. It hurts, that's all."

"Come on!"

"It's bandaged," I complained but raised my foot to show him. He placed my foot on his knee and removed the bandage.

Two of his lab coworkers came over to see what the issue was with my foot.

Get a room! I felt they were thinking.

I felt embarrassed but Hubbell seemed unperturbed.

"It's swollen," he said. "You have to put ice on it and not walk on it for a couple of days." He expertly bandaged my foot and made me put it up on another chair. He then went to the lab freezer and came back with a bag of ice.

Instead of going to my lab, I took my laptop out of my backpack and stayed next to him, pretending to work but mainly talking.

A few days later, I had a poster presentation for my Cell Biology class. I didn't think it was a big deal, so I didn't invite anyone. People came in, asked questions, then went on to other posters. Between presentations I talked to the classmate with the poster next to mine. Then I heard Hubbell's voice behind me. My body froze. I turned and saw his sideways smile.

"Aren't you going to present to me?"

My eyes beamed at him. He looked at me with such pride in his eyes! Everyone else faded away and it was just the two of us. We stared and smiled at each other.

If you could see the way you look at me, you wouldn't deny your feelings, I thought.

Now I know better. It wasn't the way he looked at me. It was the reflection of the way I looked at him.

My heart felt so big it barely fit in my chest. After the presentation, we walked together to his lab and sat side by side, not even pretending to work.

Then his phone rang and he answered it without looking at the number. His stiff voice and monosyllabic conversation made me realize who the call was from.

What am I doing? I asked myself as I rolled my chair away from his desk. I didn't want to listen to his conversation.

We walked side by side to our cars after work in complete and utter silence. Still, that night, his call came right around closing time. This time I didn't answer. Instead, the following day, Friday, I walked around the building and used a different entrance. I kept the door to my lab closed all day. After work, I left the building the same way I had come in. I also turned my cell phone off. When I got home, the phone in my apartment was ringing.

Instead of going to my room to put down my backpack, I walked into my roommate's room.

"My beach level is really low," I told her.

She looked up from her homework. "Okay," she said, understanding exactly what I meant. "Let's go."

We packed within a couple of hours, filled the car with gas and around midnight we arrived in San Diego. When highway 8 ended, we stopped at a gas station, purchased a map of the city and asked the guy behind the counter for hotel recommendations. He pointed at our newly purchased map and we headed to the Hotel District to find a place to sleep.

That turned out to be an amazing weekend. We met a couple of golden skinned and bleached haired California surfers.

"What are two girls from the Caribbean doing in San Diego?" one of them asked.

"You're spoiled," said the other one because we would not get in the water. It was too cold. Instead we sat tanning and talking to our new friends the entire day.

It started getting chilly but we all wanted to watch the sunset.

"I'm freezing but I don't want to go anywhere," the shorter of the two said, rubbing his hands over his arms. They only wore swimsuit pants. Their chests were bare. My roommate and I had a great view of muscular arms and six packs.

Both surfers were gorgeous but I fell for a freckle one of them had in his eye. I sat closer to him and allowed my roommate to claim the cutest one.

"That's because you have something beautiful in front of you," Cutest said to Freckle.

I turned to my roommate. "Are they talking about the sunset or about us?"

The surfers called later that night to invite us to hang out but before we left them they had started getting intoxicated and I wasn't up for that. Still, it was nice talking with them on the phone.

"Will I see you again?" I asked Freckle.

"Sure, if you want to visit again," he answered.

"We're leaving early tomorrow. We want to be back before dark."

"That's just the way it is, then. You live too far away."

"It sucks," I told him, yawning. We had barely slept the night before.

I knew I would never see them again. Still the short adventure had lifted my spirits. I felt powerful as I drove back to Phoenix the next day with my roommate asleep in the passenger seat. I kept the radio blaring to whatever radio station I could find on the way and fell in love with a new song that kept on coming up, *Hanging by a Moment*. I had ignored my phone all weekend long and I kept on ignoring it as it rang in my purse next to my roommate's feet. Instead I sang along to my new favorite song.

"I'm closer than when I started chasing after you."

The next morning I walked into my lab not caring what side of the building I had chosen. I did not look into Hubbell's lab. Instead I walked with my eyes looking straight forward and the dreamy smile I'd brought back from the weekend. I took out a vial of paramagnetic particles from the 4 degree refrigerator when the door opened. For a second I wondered if it was one of my two coworkers but I knew chances were higher it was someone else.

"Hey!" Hubbell said, lingering near the door. "You didn't answer your phone."

Since the phone hadn't rang that morning I assumed he meant over the weekend.

"I was out of town." I transferred the paramagnetic particles into the flask and turned back to get the rest of the reagents.

"Really? Where to?"

"To the beach."

"You went to Puerto Rico for the weekend?" he asked.

"No, I drove to San Diego with my roommate."

"You could've invited me." He took another tentative step into my lab and the door slowly closed behind him.

"You would've said 'I don't know.'" I shrugged like he usually did when he wanted to say no without really saying it.

"Maybe."

I half smiled. "That means I'm right."

He looked down, still lingering by the closed door. "You could have, I dunno, called me back at least."

I put down the bottle of saline with a louder thud than I had intended.

"Listen, I don't like this thing we're doing anymore."

He looked up at me for an instant but I could see no sign of emotion on his face other than a general regret about this conversation.

"I like you and I've made it obvious. I told you I wanted to be with you and you're not interested in me so this thing with the night calls and visits," I stopped.

"I call you because I know you're awake and I thought you liked it."

I raised my hands. "You can't blame this on me. Yes, I like your calls and I like it when you come over. That's the problem! I keep thinking you have feelings for me."

He lowered his gaze.

"If you don't, the visits are giving me the wrong signal. They have to stop."

His wide eyes were the only reaction I got this time.

"I don't want you to call me and I don't want you to visit me at night."

"You know the guys are leaving and you're my only friend now. I don't want to lose you too!"

"I know, Hubbell, I know how you feel about that." I wanted to reach out to him, to hug him and make him feel better. I knew how it hurt to say goodbye to a friend and not know if you were going to ever see them again. "But I deserve better than this."

"So I can't call you?"

"No calls, no visits. Not even here to the lab. I guess we can talk in class or when we see each other," I said pointing my hand in the general direction of the hallway.

"It's not what I want but if that's how you say it's going to be, then I have no choice," he said and ever so slowly started turning away.

I saw his sad face, his slumped shoulders, then his back. My heart twisted.

What will I regret more? I asked myself. *Doing it, or not doing it?*

"There's something I've always wanted to know," I said before closing this chapter.

Hubbell turned back to look at me. "What?"

I closed the distance between us. I held his face in my hands, and looking into his eyes, I kissed him.

I didn't have to wait for his reaction. He kissed me back, full force, and I knew. I had waited so long for a reaction from him. I knew he felt the strength of the ionic attraction I felt for him, whether he wanted to call it love or not. I wanted to know how his lips would feel. He kissed me back and didn't let go. He was always the first one to end our phone calls, before I was ready, but not this time. I ended the kiss. Then I looked into his eyes to prove I was in control. He was not.

"That's all I wanted to know," I told him. "Now you can go."

He stumbled back. "Okay." He left my lab, stunned, like a sleepwalker obeying the law.

His sleepwalking faded before midnight. He called me. As

promised, I did not answer my phone. I then heard the sound of a message and I grabbed the phone to listen to it.

"I've never felt with anyone the way I felt today," he said. "I think I'm falling in love with you."

That's what life was like right before I headed to Puerto Rico to spend a week with Allen. That's why I couldn't kiss Allen when I had the perfect chance to be with him. A wiseman once said that you understand life when you look back, but unfortunately it's late in life when you get to look back. You must live life forward.

I missed my chance with Allen because by the time that summer ended and the new semester began, Allen attended a conference in San Diego where he met a girl who was available to date him.

"You lost your chance with a really good one," my roommate said to me when Allen still came to spend time with us every time I called him. "Don't ever do that if you have a chance with him again."

His distance romance wasn't working well for Allen and by Valentine's Day, instead of flying to San Diego, he called me and asked me to go to dinner with him. We didn't go to a fancy restaurant, we went to a good fast food. We didn't dress up, we wore jeans. He didn't have eyes just for me, his eyes were downward, barely focusing on his food. I was there for him because he had always been there for me. We were friends.

By *Cinco de Mayo* they had broken up. Allen invited me to *Dos Gringos*. The restaurant had moved to a new location. They had gone from being a small kitchen and open terrace to a two-story building. They decorated the restaurant with pinatas made of papier-mache in vivid colors. The band played very loud Bob Marley music. Allen got me a margarita and we stood side by side on the second story terrace, looking down at the people.

Allen finished his margarita and went to get a Corona, then another one. I had never seen him drink like that.

"No woman no cry," he sang along with the blaring music.

"That's not really how it goes," I said, joking. "No man, no reason for women to cry."

Allen shook his head as if I didn't understand life.

The next weekend Allen went with me to a Latin party at my friend's house.

"Teach me how to dance salsa," he said.

I grabbed his hands, placed his right hand on my waist and held the other one with my right hand. I taught him how to move his hips side to side, to the rhythm of the music. He moved his legs but not his hips. Allen had no rhythm, but it didn't matter. I had seen gringos turn into dancers before.

"Get a room!" One of our bioengineering friends yelled at us.

Then I went with Allen to one of his friend's parties. While the Latin party was at a house owned by a young well-to-do realtor who loved hosting, Allen's party was in a family house, the kind of party college kids have when their parents are out of town.

Allen's younger brother and his older sister were at the party. Allen was normally frustrated by his younger brother's behavior. Both Allen and his sister had graduated *Magna Cum Laude* but their baby brother was more of a rebel without a cause. To me, he was just being a normal teenager.

Allen's sister sat on the back porch, talking to her friends. His brother sat gloomily in the living room couch, pretending to be interested in an MTV show.

Allen's sister called him.

"Will you be okay here for a bit?" he asked me.

"Of course, go!" I told him, and sat on the sofa next to his brother.

"You know, I used to watch MTV when it was a brand new channel. They only played music videos, and they didn't have that many, so they played the same ones over and over."

He looked at me out of the corner of his eye.

"They played Angel from Aerosmith a lot."

He acted like he was only half listening and rarely took his eyes from the TV but a few times he laughed at things I said, seeming to appreciate the company and my attempts to befriend him.

Out on the porch, his sister seemed to be lecturing Allen. Allen nodded with his gaze down.

Does she think I'm a bad influence? I wondered.

Allen was five years younger than me. His sister was two years older than him. Still, I didn't think I could be a bad influence on anyone.

A Princess, maybe. That's what people often described me as, but not bad.

Either way, Allen took me home later than night without telling me what his sister said.

"Do you want to come in?" I asked him.

"Por supuesto," he said.

"Do you need some water?" I asked him, out of habit.

"Sure," he said, and sat himself comfortably on my sofa. "What was that movie you were telling me about? The one about destiny?"

I loved talking and debating about destiny. "Serendipity? Yes, I have the DVD. Do you want to watch it?"

"I'd love to."

My apartment was quiet because my roommate was already asleep so we kept the volume low.

I sat on my sofa next to Allen and he put his head on my lap, like a baby. I played with his hair while we watched the movie, like I used to do with Hubbell. He laughed often and so did I.

"So you think life is predestined?" he asked when the movie ended.

"In a way," I said. "I think some things are meant to be but you can't sit in the middle of a room waiting for things to happen. You have to make them happen, to show your interest."

He sat in front of me and nodded.

Everything seemed so natural with Allen. Everything from the ASU clubs to Abuela's house. "I think we're meant to be," I said and hugged him. "Stay with me."

His smile didn't change. He stood up and I wondered if he had heard what I said. His silence felt too long.

I wanted to clarify. *I'm not offering you my body. I'm offering you my heart!*

He stood up and went near the door to get his shoes. I rose to walk him out but he sat back down, shoes in hand and slowly put them on, then came back to me and put his warm hands on my shoulders.

He looked into my eyes.

"This doesn't feel right, right now."

Then he slowly walked out of my life.

"Oh, okay," I said, as the door closed behind him. I locked the door and went into my tiny office inside my walk-in closet. I turned on the computer.

"Barbie, I can't breathe," I wrote to my best friend. "I feel like someone punched my chest so hard I can't fill my lungs with air." I sobbed uncontrollably.

I wanted that scene with Allen to poof away, but no. It wasn't an option to unfriend Allen. My parents, my brother and my younger cousin came to visit and Allen's parents invited us all to brunch at their home. I had to do a lot of pretending. I pretended I wasn't hurt, I pretended it wasn't awkward to be in the same room with him and his family.

Over time, I learned he got back together with the girl from San Diego. I learned he took her camping and taught her how to take a shower under a tree. Months later, after I had graduated, he called to let me know he had gotten engaged. I pretended to be happy for him.

Chapter 14

SURGERY

THE MORNING OF my surgery I refused to wake up early. In fact, I tried hard to fall back asleep while my mother, father and brother moved about and prepared their breakfast downstairs at my dining table.

"Lania, we're going to be late! My father called from downstairs. My Army-trained father believed we had to arrive at the airport three hours ahead of the flight.

I got up when I got tired of trying to sleep. I took a shower and put on deodorant and perfume although I had been instructed not to.

A little bit won't matter, I thought.

At the hospital, I finished the check-in process and sat in the waiting area with all the other surgery patients, sandwiched between my parents. When patients were called to the pre-surgery room, their relatives returned to the waiting room with a clear plastic bag filled with their clothes. I stood up and went into the hospital gift shop. I came back with a souvenir bag and handed it to my mother.

"What's this?" she asked.

I handed the empty backpack to her.

I pointed to the clear plastic bags other people placed in chairs next to them.

"Silly girl," she said but took it.

After about an hour, my brother asked my dad if he was ready for lunch and off they went. I felt abandoned. Tears wanted to come out but I would not let them.

A nurse finally called my name and I went into the pre-surgery room with my mother. The nurse gave us some instructions and closed the curtain around us. In the center of the space stood a narrow bed with wheels and on top of the bed a hospital gown and a disposable hat.

I could not hold back the tears anymore so I dumped myself on the bed and allowed my mother to see me cry. She hugged me but I didn't want to be hugged. I didn't want to feel what I was feeling because I didn't want to be there.

I changed into the damn gown but refused to wear the hat. I wanted my long hair all around me as the one trait of beauty I was allowed to bring into the surgery room.

A man's voice asked if he could come in. My mother opened the curtain and in came a tall, slender man with dark hair. He wore a set of generic green scrubs.

He extended his hand in greeting. "Hi, I'm Dr. Anesthesia," he said.

I shook his hand, firmly, like I had been taught years back by an engineering professor. "Nice to meet you. I'm Dr. Salas."

He winced and looked at me to see if I was joking but he saw no humor in my face. A nurse poked my arm to get an IV going and finally, my dear bald fertility doctor walked in.

I felt relieved to see him and returned the smile he gave me.

"It's all going to be okay," he assured me and I nodded.

The nurse who poked me tried to put the disposable hat on my head but I waved it away.

"Not until after the anesthesia," I said.

Speaking of the devil, Dr. Anesthesia returned and said he was going to inject the first shot into my IV. He placed a syringe on the metal tray next to my bed and filled it with a liquid from a closed vial. He then injected the liquid into my IV. In three seconds my heads felt like I had gulped down three spiced up margaritas.

"You might want to lay down," Dr. Anesthesia said.

I obeyed immediately. "Whoa! Somebody please take away my keys!"

Everybody laughed.

That's the last thing I remember before the surgery but my mother later said that I started crying and screaming as they wheeled me away.

"Please stop! I changed my mind! I don't want to lose my uterus! STOP!"

"Hey there, would you like some ice chips?" The voice sounded gentle. I knew it must be a nurse but why did she offer me ice?

I slowly opened my eyes. The room looked bright. Too bright. I saw nurses in scrubs walking around or talking to patients in beds.

Where was I? What happened to the surgery? I wondered.

"My mother?" My voice sounded hoarse and my throat hurt as if it had been sanded. "Ice," I said and the nurse placed a couple small pieces of ice in my mouth.

I heard voices and tried opening my eyes again. The nurse was not next to my bed anymore.

I must have fallen asleep, I thought.

"Ice," I said, and the friendly nurse came back and placed more ice in my mouth.

"We called your mother and told her the surgery was over and you were starting to wake up."

Satisfied, I closed my eyes.

After waking up completely they sent me to a private room. I had two floral arrangements waiting for me, a pretty one full of red flowers from my family and another one in a round smiley cup from Allen.

My bald fertility doctor came upstairs to tell me the good news that my uterus was intact and the mass didn't look malignant.

I felt better, until I went to the bathroom and saw my scar.

"Bikini scar? Has my doctor ever seen a bikini?"

The opening was from one side of my abdomen to the other, it looked red, swollen and grotesque.

"That's it for bikinis, I guess."

I went home the next day and I also got a phone call from Allen. He talked and talked about his decision to work less hours and do more mountain biking. He wanted to enjoy life while his knees still let him because who knew if in a few years his knees would start failing him again. I felt so thankful to him that I happily listened.

Two weeks later I returned to work. My closest co-worker greeted me with open arms. She visited me at home after the surgery and she was the only person at work I could confide in, and even then, I only confided after I was told I needed surgery and the idea was driving me crazy.

We had our own little offices, the size of walk-in closets but it was better than cubicle offices, and we often visited each other's office to chat.

"I'm curious," she said, looking around and closing my office door.

"About what?"

"Would you stop trying to get pregnant if you started dating again?"

I thought about it. This was too important to me. So important that I would not give up for just anyone. I would have to be in love and I would have to know I was in a committed relationship.

"No," I told her. Also, I already knew not to plan my life around a guy. "Not unless the guy proposes." *Or if the guy is Allen.*

Allen called one afternoon while I was out grocery shopping with my parents. "I'm so glad you called! I was thinking of you."

We kept the conversation short because I was in a public place with people around me, so I called him back later that day. This time he was the busy one.

"I will call you this weekend," he promised.

It took him three months to return my call. He talked and talked about his biking adventures and the races he had participated in, and I listened. I tried to interrupt his tale to talk about my own dreams but I chickened out.

He called again days later. He started talking again about his mountain biking adventures but this time I interrupted.

"I have big news."

Chapter 15

IVF

IT WASN'T EASY for me to decide to move forward with *In Vitro* Fertilization. I must have been about eight years old the first time I heard about IVF. The story about the first successful "test tube baby" was all over the news. My aunts criticized the couple and the doctors who procreated a human being against God's natural ways.

I wasn't intimidated by science. Nor was I fearful of going against God's wishes. My fear was deciding what to do with multiple embryos.

What will I do with the ones I don't get implanted? Discard them? Of course not!

My love for every child born and unborn would not allow me to think of that alternative.

Could I give my embryos to another woman who wanted to have children?

I thought of tiny adorable babies who looked like me, who shared my genes, calling someone else Momma. No, I couldn't handle that alternative either.

If I have multiple embryos, I want to give all of them a chance at life. That meant having a large family.

Before starting fertility treatments, I had estimated how much it would cost me to raise a child. Childcare in my city would cost me at least $800 per month. With my salary, I knew I could afford to have one child.

It made me appreciate my grandmother, who had raised six

children, all the more. *How did she do it? The economy wasn't any better back then!*

One time, my mother blurted in Abuela's kitchen how much money I earned at my first job. My family looked at me, surprised and silent. That was before grad school. After my PhD, I started earning over twice as much.

It would be a shame if I couldn't afford more than one child with my salary, even if I felt strongly it was the right thing to do.

I called my close friend Chiara, my traveling buddy, who shared my religious and social upbringing.

"What would you do, I asked her?"

"I don't understand. What are you worried about?"

"If I do IVF, the doctor will remove and fertilize multiple eggs. Once I have those embryos, what do I do with them? I can't afford to have a handful of children. And I can't discard the embryos either!"

She remained quiet at the other end of the line, thinking about it.

"Lania, you can't control everything! You go on and start the process. You control what you can, and you leave the rest to God."

Yes! That was the perfect answer. I still felt scared of moving forward but I had always counted on God. This should not be any different.

I already had my date for starting IVF, exactly 3 months after my surgery.

My doctor seemed reluctant to let me start that soon and I complained.

"You said 3 months!"

He didn't explain the date I selected was for implantation. The IVF process began with hormone injections one month before implantation. He took a look at my surgery, analyzed my recovery and my insistence and allowed me to proceed.

Near the end of summer, my parents returned to Puerto Rico.

My father still worked at the university there and the school year was about to start. Soon after they left, I received a large box from the online pharmacy used by my fertility clinic. I opened the box and removed multiple bags of syringes and injectable medication. Had I counted them, I would have realized there were well over 200 large syringes and about triple that number of small needles like the ones used for insulin. Instead of counting them, I immediately closed the box and waited for instructions from my fertility clinic.

The clinic said the large syringes with the impossibly wide needles were for progesterone in oil. Progesterone in oil produced a viscous solution. It was hard to push through a small needle but I would only need those later on.

The small syringes were for injecting ovulation-inducing hormones, which I needed to do on a daily basis, until my blood levels reached the right levels. I decided not to ask how they would test those blood levels. In fact, I decided to remain blissfully ignorant through most of the procedure. Just like at The Labs, I functioned on a *Need to Know* basis.

The first thing I needed to do was to learn to inject myself on my thigh.

I have done this before, I told myself. *I can do it again.*

I hated injecting myself. I only did it because of horrible cramps. Without the cramps, I needed a strong motivation.

I wasted a few needles and a vial on my first attempt because every time the needle penetrated my skin, I freaked out and involuntarily removed it. I got sweaty and dizzy. I tried injecting myself on different areas of my thighs until I found out that it was less painful to inject the fatty tissue on the outer side of my thigh.

Thank you, God, for my extra 20 pounds!

I had been a goal achiever my whole life, but this process took a completely different approach. Rather than feel overwhelmed with the needles, I decided to love each and every one of them.

Each shot will bring me closer to holding my baby in my arms.

I looked forward each day to my injection time.
One less needle in my box, one day closer to my dream.
And when I got uncomfortable with my swollen abdomen and overwhelmed with the road ahead, I would say to myself,
I can always quit tomorrow.
I thought I had read all the information my doctor and the clinic provided. Reading the protocols and experiencing the hormones were two different things. For example, the documents didn't give me information about what I would feel.

The hormones induced my ovaries to mature multiple follicles. Which meant that my ovaries were swollen. Therefore, my abdomen also felt swollen. The same abdomen that still had a sensitive surgical injury. I didn't allow anyone to touch my scar. I pushed my doctor's hand away when he tried to remove the surgical tapes. I begged him to allow them to fall on their own. I pushed my mother's hand away when she tried to do the same. I tried to remove one of the tapes while taking a shower. I held my breath and I got so dizzy I had to stop.

Now I had an expanding abdomen that hurt and felt uncomfortable all the time. I should have listened to my doctor and waited longer. A lot longer.

Or maybe not.

I still had a uterus and I planned to use it.

Dr. Jameson said it was time for my trigger shot to mature the eggs. After that, I had to go to the clinic every morning for a blood draw to find out the optimal date for retrieval. Most days, I saw the same patients in the waiting room: the fancy lady in her mid 40's, who had come to the first appointment with her business-looking husband but who now came alone, an Indian couple who never spoke a word, and an overweight lesbian couple. These women became my IVF buddies. We rarely spoke to each other, definitely not asked personal questions about why we were doing IVF but on most mornings it was enough to show each other our arms for us to understand each other.

As the hormone levels grew higher, the nurses had more trouble drawing our blood. Every morning multiple pokes were necessary to get our blood samples. All of us looked like junkies with our arms full of bruises. That and the lack of caffeine.

I started wearing long sleeve shirts to work even though the early fall in Albuquerque didn't call for it.

For the last blood draw I went to a clinic closer to home. I was mad because my retrieval date was bumped in favor of the fancy lady and the lesbian couple.

"You're younger, so the doctor said you can wait an extra day."

At the new clinic, a sweet talking phlebotomist approached me with a baby-faced student and asked me if the student could draw my blood.

"Are you sure?" I asked, pulling up my sleeves and showing them my arms.

The student stepped away from me. "Maybe not today," she said, looking at her mentor for corroboration.

The mentor nodded and asked me in a whisper, "Are you an addict?"

"No," I replied. "It's IVF."

Can I handle this one more day? I asked myself, tired and afraid of what awaited me. *Yes, I can. I can always quit tomorrow.*

The morning of my retrieval I woke up in good spirits. I apologized to the clinic staff about my temper flare the previous day.

"It's expected, darling. It's the hormones talking," my favorite nurse, Miss America, said.

She instructed me to change into the usual gown and lay on the table.

I loved my doctor more than ever because he brought me a new anesthesiologist to get me down for the retrieval. Some RE clinics didn't use anesthesia for the retrieval. I felt so glad mine did.

Out of the 17 eggs that were nicely maturing during the previous check, they were able to remove 12 from my ovaries.

Miss America said I might experience cramping. "It's okay for you to take some acetaminophen," she said. "Call the office tomorrow to find out how many eggs fertilized. Your embryo implantation will be on day 3 or day 5 after fertilization, depending on how well your embryos develop. For a young woman like you, it will probably be on day 5."

My family eagerly awaited news of the IVF results, even the family members who were against my decision, like my aunt, who called to say she was against it, and Abuela, who also called me and said the same thing. I learned Abuelo had said,

"She has a good head over her shoulders. She knows what she's doing."

I loved the men in my family.

The next day I called the clinic and found out I had 8 embryos.

"Abuelo, even you will be in charge of one of the babies," my aunt said.

I have fertilized embryos. There's no going back, I can only move forward. I will not quit tomorrow, or any other day.

Just like Miss America predicted, my embryos looked nice and healthy on day 3, so I was scheduled for implantation on day 5.

On implantation day, my abdomen still felt sore but I felt happy. I hugged the wonderful staff on my way to the procedure room.

"What is your PhD in?" Dr. Jameson asked in front of all the staff. It had become a favorite question of his.

"Bioengineering," I replied, and the staff "Ooh-ed" and "Ah-ed".

My doctor showed me a picture of two golden circles and informed me they were the best looking embryos. They looked to me like gold coins, so I nicknamed them that. My two gold coins. He said a third embryo had made it to day 5 but it didn't look as well developed as the two in the picture.

"How many would you like implanted?" he asked.

I had read about statistics and recommendations for women my age and older. "One or two," I answered.

Dr. Jameson nodded. "For your age that's what I recommend too. One or two. Not three."

"Not three," I agreed. I looked at the picture of my two perfect gold coins and I had my answer. "Two. Definitely two."

"Do you want to freeze the third embryo for future consideration?"

"Yes! Definitely yes."

"Okay," he said. "Call tomorrow to ask how the freezing process went."

I went home and took a long nap on my sofa.

My babies are inside me now.

I held the picture of my two gold coins next to my heart. I thought about their little souls. In my thoughts, I reached out my arms to them in heaven and they reached down their arms to me. We held on tight.

I sang to them one of my favorite songs from Menudo, *Por Amor*.

"You were born from love." I knew that from then on, every time I told my children their story, I would begin it with those words.

The next day, I called the clinic to ask about my remaining embryo.

"There was nothing to freeze," Dr. Jameson said. "The third embryo didn't look healthy enough to freeze. It stopped developing."

Uh oh. If this doesn't work, I have nothing. Or maybe this is God's way of helping me solve my fears.

Later, I learned none of my IVF buddies had embryos on implantation day. I could still hold on to hope over the next two weeks, but they had gone home empty handed.

Chapter 16

I THINK I'M FALLING

I REMEMBER THE time I told Hubbell my plans. "I don't need a man. I can have children by myself."

He looked at me, frowning. "You can't mean by insemination." He made it sound like something that was beneath me and an insult to his male ego.

He often said he liked it that I was so independent, so there, I threw it at him. My most independent self.

It had happened between the time he had told me he thought he loved me and the long semester he took to conclude he needed to break up with his girlfriend.

"What would you say to your best friend if a guy treats her like you're treating me?" I asked Hubbell one night in my apartment.

"Fuck him!" he said. "I mean, he's not worth it."

"Then why?"

He shrugged. "I dunno. She doesn't have anywhere else to go."

I didn't want to be spiteful. I liked the girl. He had brought her over to my place a couple of times. His roommates too and mine. We all hung out together like one big happy family or like an episode of *Friends*.

It was the night of my 25th birthday. My roommate gave me a satin nightgown in white with delicate floral design, the kind I only wore when I was alone in the apartment. She had gone to bed early that night and suspecting I would have company later on, I wore it anyway.

Hubbell called. "I'm outside."

I opened the door.

"Wow," he said when he saw me. He touched the silky strap of my nightgown with his fingers. "I like this."

I walked back to my room and he followed me. I went back to my bed. He took his shoes off and got in bed with me. My radio, as usual, was on. A new song played.

"So you sailed away…"

"My song," I said.

He laughed softly and turned to face me. "You have a lot of songs."

"But you've never found one for me," I complained.

"I'm not that romantic. You know I don't know how to be affectionate."

"You don't, huh?" I played with his wavy hair, a move he had described before as *the safest place on earth*. "Kiss me!" I demanded.

He laughed a deep murmured laugh. He closed the small gap between us, put his hand on my bare back and kissed me.

"You scare me," he said between kisses.

"Why?"

"You probably want to get married soon."

I shrugged. "Maybe about two years after graduation."

"That doesn't sound bad."

"You're the one person I never want to say goodbye to."

I kissed him again and he lowered his hand further down and inside my nightgown. *Nothing* happened between us from then on.

Still, I didn't know if I had him. If his mind was on anyone else, until *that night*.

That night we went out with friends from grad school. My roommate and a friend of hers joined us, and one of the new bioengineering girls. Hubbell brought one of his roommates, one of the ones that liked me. We went to a piano bar. Since the guys rarely dressed up like I had envisioned a formal piano lounge with classical music. Instead the piano bar had two back to back grand pianos with musicians playing modern favorites like *Piano Man* and *Great Balls of Fire*.

I wore a long summer dress. My roommate and the other girls also wore skirts or little black dresses. Mine, of course, was red.

At every other outing we had, Hubbell and I had kept some distance so as to not make our relationship too obvious to our crowd. That night we kept no distance. Upon entering the bar, Hubbell had grabbed a little piece of paper. Since I didn't know the purpose, I hadn't gotten one myself. Hubbell wrote something on his paper and gave it to me.

"Go, hand it to the musician or place it in the cup on his piano." I had seen him write it, so I knew what it said.

I crossed the center of the bar. The waxed wooden floor felt slippery with my high heels and I had to hold on to the piano, once I reached it, not to fall. The glass cup on the piano looked empty and the musician held out his hand to receive my piece of paper as he finished the notes of his current song with his left hand. He read the two words and asked me to remind him who it was from.

"Elton John," I said. He nodded, and searched through his book of song. I went back to my group.

I beamed on my way back and Hubbell smiled. He began singing with the piano man in his deep husky voice. "Blue jean baby..."

"Are you happy?" Hubbell's roommate asked me.

Instead of answering I hugged Hubbell as he continued to sing, "Hold me closer Tiny Dancer..."

"I thought so," his roommate said. Since the music played loud, he got closer to my ear to say something.

Hubbell turned, annoyed, and pushed him away.

My blood drained. I stepped in between them and tried to

spread them apart with my arms, but it felt like trying to move away two bulldozers. They didn't flinch. They looked at each other with the alpha-male look of competition.

They're going to fight! I had no choice but to move away and let them handle it. I had heard of guys fighting for the same girl. It had happened to a friend from high school and I had felt jealous. I never would have dreamed of two men fighting for me. Right at that moment, though, I didn't feel flattered. Only later. At that moment I felt scared of the possible fight. I turned around to call our group of friends and ask for help. It must have been this move that made them come to their senses. They backed away from each other and became civilized people again. It all had happened in a matter of seconds, and I quickly realized that although some people had stared, no one from our group had noticed the momentary conflict.

When the night was over, we went back to Hubbell's house. I felt tired and lay on his leather sofa. Hubbell leaned on the back of the sofa and looked down at me.

"I'm ready to go home, Lania, are you coming?" my roommate asked me.

Although I wanted to stay around, the house was still full of people and I had never stayed with him. It was always him coming to my place. I said my goodbyes and left with my roommate.

Not five minutes had passed when Hubbell called my cell phone. I answered it, still in a daze.

"Can you look out at the moon?" he asked.

I had seen it but I looked out of the car again. It was a gigantic bright desert moon.

"I see it," I told him, knowing he was out looking at it too. *I finally have him*, I said to myself. *He's all mine.*

We lasted a little while. Then he had to spend a summer in Florida training on new research procedures.

"You should come stay with me," he said. "You love Florida."

"Maybe I will," I said. Chiara had just moved to Florida and we hadn't traveled together since she visited Arizona. I called her and we made plans. I decided to stay with Chiara instead than with Hubbell. He could travel south to Palm Beach or meet us halfway in Orlando for a weekend.

He traveled first and called me to let me know he had arrived. Then he stopped calling. The first weekend, I waited for him to call me. I waited until closing time in Florida and his call never came, so I called him at 3am.

"Take it easy, I've been busy," he said, but didn't call the next day or the next.

I received a package from my mother with a new dress and other beautiful clothes I could wear in Florida. I tried some pieces on and while looking in the mirror, I heard an instant message. I went into my closet office and looked into Messenger.

"Hey," he wrote.

"Hi!" I wrote back, trying to bite back the *finally*. "What's going on?"

"Trying to get used to the new place. I don't have a car here and I depend on people to offer rides on the weekend to the supermarket."

Bullshit, I thought. "What's her name?"

typing...

typing...

"Say it!" I wrote.

"Say what?"

"You've been dragging me forever and I get mad because I know what you're doing but I always take you back. If you don't want to be with me then end it now."

typing...

"End what? There's nothing to end. You've been nothing but a mistake and a fling that shouldn't off happened."

I had lost count of how many "off's" I had edited from his school papers. I knew for sure it was him on the other side. His words felt so much more cutting than anything I thought he could say.

Not even a friend for the last three years? This time, I knew I would never go back.

I went swimming to the beach and the weather felt so very perfect. I had a round float and I got on it. It felt peaceful. I used my arms and feet to move further away from shore and looked back at the people on the sand getting smaller and smaller. I heard voices warning me about tides but I didn't want to give up my fun. Instead, I daringly kept on swimming further and further from shore. It felt wonderful, so I closed my eyes to enjoy the breeze. Soft waves playfully crashed against the tube and splashed my body. I could taste the salty water droplets that fell on my face. I think I must have dozed because after a while the waves felt sharper and stronger. I opened my eyes and saw the tide had turned. Gray clouds covered the previously clear blue sky. Thunder roared and being far from shore didn't feel safe anymore. I wanted to go back but the waves felt sharper and stronger. I swam with all my strength but the tide kept pushing me back. I felt tired and out of breath, wondering if I would make it. With a sudden jerk, I landed on sand. I woke up from that same sudden jerk, and realized I lay safely on the bed in my apartment. I had felt safe on the sand too.

The dream felt too real. I went to get a Coke from my fridge and got on my computer to tell Barbie about it. As I opened up Messenger, I heard the sound of an incoming message.

Hubbell? I wondered, but it wasn't him, it was his roommate, the one with who he almost fought at the piano bar. I wanted to know if he'd heard from Hubbell but I refused to be the one to ask. Instead, I told him about my dream.

"What do you think it means?" he asked.

Oh! His question prompted a sudden realization. *I had been swimming against the current, but it had felt wonderful in the beginning.*

"So?" he asked.

"Nothing," I answered.

"Coward!"

Ha! "If I were a coward, I wouldn't have swum so deep." *I might feel hurt now but I will land safely from this too.*

I still traveled to Florida and managed to have fun thanks to my friend Chiara. We went to the parks, to the malls and to beachside restaurants at night. When I returned to Arizona, nothing felt the same.

Annie, a friend from church convinced me of going to a retreat with her to Prescott. Annie and I had become friends in that same retreat two years before. While ASU had more cactus than trees, Prescott was covered by tall pine trees. My cell phone couldn't get a single line of signal in Prescott.

The retreat area consisted of several small log cabins surrounding a larger main cabin. Most activities took place in the main cabin, including all meals and mass. The small cabins were the sleeping quarters, with six bunk beds per cabin for a capacity of twelve people. All cabins to the right housed the men and the ones to the left housed the women. Only the main cabin had restrooms and showers so if you needed to go in the middle of the night, you had to remember to carry your own flashlight.

During my first retreat I had seen other students crying and wondered what they cried about. To me, their tears seemed fake and melodramatic. This time, I was the one crying during every single group session. Initially, I tried to remain quiet, keeping my thoughts to myself. I listened to everyone else's stories. Soon people around me started noticing the screaming in my silence. They invited me to participate and asked me questions. As soon as I tried to open my mouth, the flood gates opened.

"What's wrong with you?" my friend Annie asked, privately, after a session.

I told her about Hubbell. She listened attentively.

"I thought he was my best friends and that I was falling in love with him. For him I must have been the other girl, the rebound. I let him use me. He walked all over me and I allowed it to happen for so long."

Annie hugged me without judgement. Or if she judged me, she never mentioned it and it didn't weigh on our friendship. We took a walk together. Then I told her I felt tired and wanted to nap instead of going to the next session.

After the session, she came back to check on me. I had just awoken and I felt better.

"Let me take a picture of you," she said.

"I'm not wearing any makeup and my face is probably still red."

"You're fine," she said, rolling her eyes.

I sat on the bottom bunk and she quickly snapped it, before I changed my mind. I still have the picture. I kept it because I looked pretty in it, but although I smiled for the picture, the smile didn't reach my eyes. I kept it as a reminder that I would never allow myself to be treated like a doormat again.

As the sun started to fall that day, we had an arts and crafts activity in the main cabin. The priest gave us a blank puzzle, the size of a 5x7 inch photo. First, we had to say a prayer and ask for guidance. Then we had to go out in nature, by ourselves, and listen to the answer.

I asked for water. I missed the beach and although I knew that was too much to pray for in the middle of Arizona, I thought I might be able to find a river or a pond somewhere. I went out and saw other students going in all directions. I started walking uphill in the direction of the mountains but then changed my mind, remembering that two years ago I had hiked that way with other students and had seen animals and beautiful scenery but not water.

I walked downhill a bit and turned around, realizing I had no idea what to look for. In Puerto Rico, if I wanted to find the ocean I looked for palm trees. If I wanted to look for a river or sweet water, I looked for bamboo trees. I was surrounded by pine trees, so high that even if I looked up, that's what I saw. In fact, the air smelled so strongly of pine trees, that taking a deep breath and trying to sniff around for water, only hurt my nostrils. I walked for about fifteen more minutes, then, I almost gave up.

"Try looking down."

It wasn't a voice. It was a feeling. It was a bit too ridiculous, but I looked down anyway. There, right next to my foot, I saw the thinnest stream of water.

How didn't I notice it before? Where does it come from? It hasn't been raining. The earth is dry. I bent down and paid closer attention now and realized that beneath rocks, leaves and pine needles, the little stream had traveled hidden next to me for a while. Now all I had to do was follow it down. I smiled for the next ten minutes, certain I would find it because the little stream grew bigger and more obvious. Then, beyond the noise of the wind blowing pine branches, I heard the sound of a large stream of water. Sure enough, not much further I saw the river.

I want to see a waterfall! I said now, smiling to myself and daring the heavens. The river grew larger and larger and I knew if I walked further I would get my waterfall, but the sun was starting to set and I still had to make it back to the cabin. I knew I would be a bit late, but that would be okay.

Back at the main cabin, everyone else had busied themselves drawing their puzzles, talking and laughing.

Annie lifted her head as soon as I walked in. "There you are! I was about to send a search party!"

I heard the humor in her voice and the smiles of those around her. I sat next to her and on my white canvas puzzle, I drew my little stream of water getting bigger until it formed a large river. I decided to include the waterfall.

I have never been an artist, but my little watercolor turned out okay.

"What does it mean?" Annie and the other students asked.

I told them my story of finding the stream next to my foot and then the river.

"There's a river here?" Annie asked. "I've never seen it."

Some of the other students had seen it. I had seen some of them praying in that area.

I dismantled my little puzzle and found the full meaning of my story as I started to put it back together. Halfway through, I lifted a single piece.

"Life is like a puzzle," I said to the others. "If you try to force a piece where it doesn't belong, the overall picture will not look as great."

One late summer day in 2003, before the crowds arrived at ASU for the Fall semester, I saw a bioengineering friend who often hung out with us. I waived and he approached me.

"Did you hear the news?"

"Yes," I sad, thinking he referred to one of the guys from the house, who had gotten engaged.

Apparently, he wanted to tell me. "Hubbell got engaged."

"Hubbell?"

Soon after, I found out he had gotten married, years before his graduation. I graduated ahead of him. When my friends started throwing goodbye parties and dinners for me, I thought about inviting him.

What the heck, I'm leaving anyway. Then I remembered I didn't want to ever say goodbye to him, so I didn't.

Chapter 17

ULTRASOUND

"LANIA, WHAT IF it doesn't work?" Barbie asked on Messenger.

Most days I felt afraid it would not work. If the eight IUI's I had before my surgery hadn't worked, what made me think IVF would be different? Still, I had a tiny flame of hope, maybe a little mustard seed, a *knowing* that this time it would work.

"I believe it will," I replied. "I have a good feeling this time."

Sometimes, I didn't trust the flame, the seed or the knowing.

I didn't want to test too early. If I tested too early, the injected hormones would result in a false positive test. I didn't want to get my hopes up by a false test. Still, waiting the full 2ww without testing was like having a box of chocolates while on a diet. I tested three days early.

Nothing. No pink lines. Not even a trace of the injected hormones. No trace of a possible pregnancy. Nothing at all.

I felt crushed. I cried and cried. It hadn't worked. I had gone through a year of fertility treatments and I had nothing to show for it.

Once again, my mother, who had returned to help with the injectable progesterone in oil, became my pillar.

"You don't know for sure. You can test again tomorrow, or you can wait for the blood test."

Three days. I could wait three days. Three days can feel like three eternities for a woman waiting to find out if she is pregnant.

I had an awards dinner with my group of writers the first

of those three days. That would help eliminate one of the three eternities. Writing was a lifelong hobby I never had time for until I moved to Albuquerque. I had taken a Continuous Education creative writing class in the evenings, then I had participated in a writing marathon called NaNoWriMo and from there a few of us had continued meeting on a weekly basis to exchange and edit chapters of our novels. Every year we participated of a local competition and if one of us were nominated for a prize we would attend the awards dinner.

I wore a dress, put on makeup, chose my jewelry and drove myself to the event. I met my writer friends there.

The dinner began with a giant chocolate fountain and assortments of strawberries and other fruits.

Totally sinful! I thought. *What a great way to spend my time!*

The winners were announced and we applauded. Waiters served the first course, which consisted of a cool and creamy Caesar salad. I ate it while chatting with my friends. The waiters replaced my salad plate with the main course, rice pilaf and chicken breast. I didn't like chicken breast too much, I found it fibrous and dry but it tasted good with the rice. I loved all kinds of rice.

The dinner ended with a large piece of chocolate cake and coffee. I said yes to coffee, although I knew I would only sip it. The chocolate cake, though, tasted delicious.

"Lania?"

It's a big piece of chocolate cake, I thought halfway through it. *It's too good not to eat, though.*

"Lania."

How come I still have space for the chocolate cake? Didn't I just eat a four-course meal?

"Lania!"

"What?" I looked up from my chocolate cake, startled.

My friends laughed.

"Is the chocolate cake good? You seem to be engrossed in it."

I laughed, knowing if I could blush I would definitely be blushing. "Yes, it's good." *But I never eat this much! Could I be pregnant?*

I woke up early the day of my blood test. I had made it through the 2-week-wait but I wasn't going to make it to the blood test without an idea of the result. I needed to be prepared. If I had to cry, I would do it in private, not on the phone when I heard the bad news. I grabbed a pregnancy test and went to the bathroom. I had held on all night without using the bathroom so I would have the most concentrated sample in the morning. Please, God, help me, I said as I waited a full minute with my eyes closed. Then I waited longer. I refused to peek until a few minutes passed.

I held my breath as I turned to look at the test on the bathroom counter. I didn't feel prepared. I had been devastated so many times already. I didn't know if I could handle it again.

I braced myself and opened my eyes.

There on the counter, I looked to find the control line. Next to it I saw a slightly fainter, but clearly visible, second line. Two pink lines.

Oh, my God! I smiled.

Could I really hope? No! Not yet. I needed the blood test. I would not dare hope until I got the results from the blood test.

I got my blood drawn and went to work but I couldn't focus on science. After lunch I called the clinic.

"We don't have the results yet, but we will call you by the end of the day," Miss America said.

"I don't know if I can wait that long. Please, try to find out for me."

I felt her smile. "I understand. I'll see what I can do."

She called me an hour later.

"Say it fast, please."

"Okay. Your results say you're positive. Congratulations! You're pregnant."

Thank you, God. I felt relief and happiness but in a dazed kind of way.

Is it really happening?

Careful, I thought. *Pregnancies can be tricky.*

Then I got hung up on the word pregnancy.

I am pregnant. I am expecting a baby. I placed my hand over my still swollen and sore abdomen.

My baby!

The next day, it was time to call my grandma. She had found out through bits and pieces of conversation from family members, including my mother, whom I had sworn to secrecy. Not that my mother has ever been able to keep a secret.

According to my mother, this is how it happened:

My parents went to visit my grandmother and as usual, they sat out on the balcony.

"I had a dream last night," Abuela said, "in which a little bird came to sit on my lap. Suddenly the bird turned into a baby. A cherubic baby. I held the baby in my arms, close to my heart and I felt full of love for this little baby."

Then she eyed my mother.

"Is Lania pregnant?" she asked.

My mother said she shrugged. She didn't want to give away my secret but she didn't want to lie to her mother either. "No, she's not pregnant."

"Is she trying to get pregnant," Abuela insisted.

My mother turned her head from side to side, wanting to say no, but shrugged instead.

I can visualize the smile my mother didn't mention.

"How is she doing it?" Abuela asked.

So my mother gave her all the details.

That same day, Abuela called me. "I don't like what you're doing."

My parents raised me to never talk back to Abuela, or to my elders. I didn't talk back to Abuela. I closed my lips and listened.

"The church teaches us... what will the Priest say... what will people think... you have always been such a nice girl... my pride and joy...you should conform to God's plan."

If I had told Abuela the story about the Immaculate Conception and the sign, she might have changed her mind, because the story fascinated her years later when I told Abuelo and Abuela on our way to their doctor's appointment.

"You should give testimony at church about your story!"

I didn't at that moment because it didn't matter what she said. I knew she loved me and I knew my mind was set and neither my grandmother nor anyone else was going to change it. Being a mother was part of my life's purpose. If I had a calling from God, that was it.

Abuela began calling me more frequently. "Any news yet?"

"Not yet," I said month after month.

After my positive test, I called her. "Abuela, ya!"

"Hija!" she said. "Already, what?"

"Already, already."

"You're pregnant?" she asked.

"Yes!"

"Glory to God in the Heavens! I have prayed so much for you."

After implantation, every night my mother administered a shot of the progesterone in oil and every time she felt so bad for me, she cried.

"I can't believe you're willing to go through with this," she'd say.

I didn't count the number of nights I got those horrible shots with the large diameter needle and the viscous solution that took so much effort to push through and into my muscle, but my mother counted them.

Seventy five.

Although they were painful, I didn't mind the shots. I held on to them for dear life. They kept my baby inside me.

At six weeks I had my first ultrasound. I invited my mother and my sister-in-law, Kim, to be with me. I had finally joined the group of Single Mothers by Choice, which had members from all over the world and whose purpose was to communicate by email and exchange advice. I knew inviting a close friend or relative to the ultrasounds was common practice.

Although I looked forward to the ultrasound, I also felt nervous.

"I'm afraid I might not be pregnant anymore," I had told my surgeon friend over the phone.

"Why? Have you had any bleeding?" she asked.

"Only minor implantation bleeding," I replied.

"Then, of course you're pregnant! Women don't pee their babies out!"

My wonderful bald doctor performed the ultrasound. "Let's see how you're doing. How many did we implant?" he asked.

"Two," I said.

"And you had a positive pregnancy test, correct?"

"Yes," I answered. I smiled from ear to ear.

"They don't always implant. You might only have one baby," he warned.

I held my breath, looking for anything that looked like a baby on the monitor.

"I found it!" Dr. Jameson said.

I could see a little ball darker than the rest of the gray image.

"That's the sac," he pointed to the ball or balloon area. "And that's the baby." This time he pointed to a lighter dot close to the wall of the sac.

"I will print you a picture," Miss America said, smiling at me.

Dr. Jameson continued his search. "Ah, and here's the other one! Twins. You're having twins!" He looked from me to my mother. "Is that good news?"

My mother's hands covered her mouth. She looked at me and uncovered her smile. She kissed me and from up close, I could see a tear shining in her eye. "It's great news."

"Keep on looking, there's gotta be another one!" Kim said and we all laughed.

"No, let's leave it at two!" I said. "That's enough."

"Are you happy with twins?" Miss America asked.

"I had two implanted," I thought, but I had always planned on one baby. "Two cribs, two car seats, two college tuitions and a minivan."

They all laughed, especially Dr. Jameson. He seemed to truly enjoy this part of his job.

"Two cribs, two car seats, two college tuitions and a minivan," I said when giving the news to my father and brother.

"Two cribs, two car seats, two college tuitions and a minivan," I said when giving the news to Abuela and Abuelo.

I repeated the same phrase when giving the news to my aunts and uncles, and cousins, and to my closest friends. They all laughed.

"Two cribs, two car seats, two college tuitions and a minivan," I said to myself before going to bed that night. I did not sleep at all.

Chapter 18

GRADUATION

AT NINE WEEKS, I had another ultrasound.

"Do I still have twins?" I immediately asked. "Are they okay?"

I worried all the time between doctor checkups. The worry never completely went away.

"Welcome to Motherhood," my friend Chiara said. "You'll learn what it means to wear your heart on your sleeve."

My RE thought his job was done. "Congratulations, you have graduated from fertility care. If you don't have a gynecologist who can supervise your pregnancy, I can refer you to one."

"What?" I asked. "I thought you were going to be with me until I gave birth."

"I haven't delivered a baby in years and I probably forgot how. With that surgery on your uterus, you will go straight to C-section. I will indicate that in my letter to your new doctor. Don't even try to convince him to let you give birth naturally."

I nodded. He had given me that warning before I'd signed the surgery papers. If given the choice, I believe I would have opted for a C-section anyway.

"You've graduated," Miss America said. She gave me a big warm hug, like she did at the end of every appointment. All the nurses in Dr. Jameson's clinic hugged their patients. I didn't get the same loving atmosphere at my next clinic and I missed it dearly.

I found out my Gypsy OB/Gyn didn't deliver babies either.

"It takes great strength to pull out a baby. I don't have that strength in my arms anymore," she said.

Dr. Jameson wanted to refer me to another woman doctor, then he remembered a Puerto Rican colleague of his. I thought it would be a good choice and agreed to go with him.

Nausea started the morning I opened the freezer and had to shut it closed immediately because the smell of frozen meat felt overpowering. I had grilled asparagus and broccoli the night before and tried to eat it again for lunch that day but their strong metal smell made me stay away from most vegetables the rest of my pregnancy. Actually, I stayed away from asparagus and broccoli the rest of my life.

I thought I would be the kind of pregnant woman who ate nutritious food, including veggies and drank milk every day. I did until the day I opened the freezer. After that I could not even drink water. In fact, I stayed away from the kitchen altogether. Luckily, my mother stayed with me. Since she had experienced nine months of vomiting during both her pregnancies, she understood and had no problem taking over the cooking. The problem was finding out what I could eat. Fruits tasted wonderful and I purchased boxes of oranges and trays of mango (the hard and sour pieces, not the ripe ones), whole pineapples and honeydews. Half a honeydew would make a meal.

I could eat a cheese sandwich or a ham sandwich. I could not eat a ham and cheese sandwich. Flavors intensified. My mother cooked chicken and ham soup once and I couldn't eat it.

"What can I make you?" she asked frustrated.

White rice and broth tasted okay, as long as the broth only had one meat and she only added salt and fresh garlic to season it with. Even then, the amount I served on my plate would not have satisfied a toddler.

I stopped eating my favorite foods, including Nutella, my favorite chocolate. "My babies think it's poison."

It wasn't only flavors. All my senses intensified. I felt like the vampire Louis in *Interview with the Vampire* when he changed from human to vampire. I could smell the leaves as they changed color that Fall. Walking to work after gardeners mowed the lawn felt like torture. I had to hold my breath until I arrived in the building.

Morning sickness lasted until at least 10:00 AM. I could not look at the computer monitor for more than ten minutes without getting major nausea and headaches. Curiously, the smell of bacteria culture media made me nauseous some days and gave me cravings on others.

Luckily, by then I had started to participate more in the SMC, or Single Mothers by Choice group. I sent them an email with the subject line, *OMG, the nausea!*

Many replied back with wonderful advice.

"I leave saltine crackers on my bedside table and before I fully open my eyes, I start biting little pieces of the crackers."

"Try Preggie Pop Drops. I swear by them."

"The nausea is due to increased hormone levels. I am also expecting twins and my hormones are twice what they usually are for women who are only carrying one baby. My doctor prescribed Zofran for nausea and Pepcid for acid reflux, which gets really bad at night," Brooke said.

I learned Brooke lived in Arizona and she got pregnant with IVF twins three months before me. She became my pregnancy buddy. To this day she is my strongest SMC friend.

I took Brooke's advice and asked Dr. Mendez if I could use Pepcid.

"Yes," he said. "Take it at night and in the morning."

"But it's a 24-hour pill."

"That dose is not enough for pregnant women," he assured me. He also prescribed Zofran.

Unlike my mother and Brooke, who vomited every day unless they took their meds, I only vomited three times and took a total of 6 Zofran pills during my pregnancy, although I always carried it around, just in case. Two of the three times, I had eaten *enchiladas* at a local restaurant. I should have known better! The third time was my big fall from grace. It happened at work.

My hemoglobin levels dropped and Dr. Mendez prescribed iron once a day. He forgot to say I should take it with a full stomach. I took the first pill in the morning and went to work. As soon as I arrived, I felt nauseous and went for a walk to get some air. The cool autumn air helped a bit but didn't take the nausea away. I walked further from the office, to the other side of the building. Suddenly, a wave of nausea came. I turned to head to the restroom but the motion of turning made things worse. I almost threw up on my shoes. I took two steps and another wave of nausea came. Two more steps and another. I think I threw up about six times. When I felt confident that it was over, I headed to work and noticed, for the first time, that all the walls on the building were made of glass. I wondered how many people saw me. I had not announced my pregnancy at work yet.

By the time I had my second appointment with Dr. Mendez, I had lost five pounds. Luckily, my cravings started after week 17. People often ask what weird cravings I had. For me, anything I could put mustard on, tasted good. Also, my favorite midnight snack became Brie with raspberry jam.

"Mmm...it makes sense," another SMC replied when I emailed about this craving. I guess it only makes sense to pregnant women.

Chapter 19

GENETIC TESTING

THE NAUSEA STARTED subsiding after week 17, around the same time my Perinatal appointments started. Dr. Jameson had referred me to Perinatal Care because of my age.

"I thought the risk was for women 35 or older."

"Not for twins," he said. "And you also had IVF."

Sitting at yet another waiting area, I realized I didn't know how perinatals differed from regular OB/Gyns or why I needed to be under the care of both. As hard-headed as I am, I didn't ask. The first specialist to see me was a lady, somewhat older than me, but nowhere near retirement age.

"How are you doing so far?" was the first question she asked.

"Great," I answered, "except I need to pee every five minutes."

"Isn't that something?" she said, nicely. "You're pregnant and you need to pee!" She understood my request and I excused myself.

When I returned to her office, she held up a set of note cards in her hands.

"Do you know what these are?" She presented the first card, a picture of wriggly X-shaped wormy structures.

Is this what Perinatals are about? "They're chromosomes," I answered, feeling slightly insulted. "Actually, they're a cartoon depiction of chromosomes." I wanted to say more. *Chromosomes contain genetic information and are made of deoxyribonucleic acid or DNA in the shape of a double helix, and so on.*

"Very good," she praised, switching to the next card. It was a picture of a baby with half a chromosome in pink and the other half in blue. "Chromosomes contain the genetic information we pass on to our children. One set comes from the mother and the other from the father."

*Give me those cards and I'll teach **you** your class!*

She continued with me fuming inside. When she finished with all her cards she put them down and opened a large binder that had been sitting on her lap.

"These are the tests we offer to help you make an informed decision about your pregnancy." She showed me tabulated information and data for their different tests.

I blinked.

"And the good news is, all these tests are covered by your insurance."

I suddenly felt in the presence of a salesperson. My initial reaction was to politely decline but a sudden memory invaded my brain.

When I was in my last year of high school, my mother's shift at the hospital ended close to midnight and the road back home was dangerous, especially in the dark. I stayed awake to know she was home safe and opened the door for her. Often, we would sit and chat over a midnight snack and my mother would tell horror stories of events at work, like a baby being born without a trachea.

I stared at the perinatal binder and flipped through the possible tests.

"Not amniocentesis," I said to the perinatal doctor. I wasn't going to poke into my babies' amniotic sac. These perinatal doctors were crazy if they thought I had come this far to risk my pregnancy. "But I will choose one of these tests."

I asked detailed questions about each, then settled on one that required a non-invasive ultrasound to measure the babies' bones and a test of my blood that would be sent out to a genetic diagnostics company.

Pleased with my choice, I went to the reception desk to make an appointment for the genetic screening.

For some reason, my mother insisted on going with me to the appointment.

"It's not necessary," I told her. "It's just another ultrasound, a poke and then I can return to work."

"Okay," she replied, but a few minutes later she changed her mind again and got in the car with me.

At the perinatals, I was led to an ultrasound room with a technician and another perinatal doctor, this time a young man. He came, introduced himself then left, allowing the technician to perform the ultrasound.

The technician squirted warm gel on my abdomen but when she placed the probe on my skin my reflex was to push it away. It felt uncomfortable. She looked at me worried rather than mad, so I showed her my scar. She gasped.

"How long ago was that?"

I had difficulty estimating when exactly my pregnancy began, so I simply said, "About five months ago."

She thought about it, "It should be healed."

"It wasn't healed when it began to stretch during IVF so it still feels sore."

She promised to be more careful but I still had to hold myself from pushing her probe through the entire procedure. With clenched teeth, I distracted myself by looking at the ultrasound monitor.

"This must be Baby B," she said, angling the probe and pointing higher on the monitor.

Twins were referred to as Baby A, the one closer to the birth canal, and thus the one that would be born first, or Baby B, the one further up, or the second to be born.

I was surprised to see how well-formed my baby looked. I could distinguish his head from his body and some of his limbs as the grayscale image shifted around on the monitor.

As the doctor had explained, the technician measured the head, the limbs and the opening of the spinal cord. Then she switched to Baby A. She once again measured the baby's bones but this time I noticed she kept repeating the spine measurement.

"Hold on a moment," she said, leaving the room.

My mother and I looked at each other questioningly. Then I heard a distinct voice in my head. "My babies are perfectly okay. Get up and leave! This is all drama."

The technician returned with the perinatal doctor in tow and showed him the data she had captured on my Baby A's spine. They exchanged a few words and he nodded in agreement with her assessment. He turned to me.

"Did you complete your preliminary appointment with our Genetic Counselor?"

"Is that what she was?" I asked in return. "Why?"

"Your ultrasound shows a wider than normal neural tube on Baby A. It still depends on the results of the blood test but this is an indication of possible birth defects."

That was a hard blow to my chest. "Like which ones?" My mother looked from me to the doctor with a pained expression.

"One of the possibilities is Turner Syndrome."

"Turner Syndrome is a female with a single X chromosome. She can have a normal life but will have fertility problems," I stated, not to show off but for corroboration.

The doctor nodded.

I can deal with that, I thought, so I shrugged. "When the time comes, I can help her with fertility options."

"Yes," he agreed. "Sounds like you know about this."

"What are the other possibilities?"

"We often see this with Trisomy 21 cases."

"Oh," I said, feeling another sudden blow to my chest. "Down Syndrome."

The doctor nodded again. "You're how far along?" he asked, referring to my chart.

"Almost eighteen weeks."

"By the time you get your blood results back, it might be too late for you to get an abortion in New Mexico but you can still go to another State."

Shock must have registered on my face as I stared at him.

"Would you like to talk to our Genetic Counselor?"

I laughed. "No." *Hell, no!*

But the test wasn't over. They drew my blood while I stood motionless, surprised that unfrozen blood came out of my veins. I pushed all thoughts and feelings away, as far away from me as possible, while the technician also poked my finger and placed some drops of blood on a card.

"This test will be sent out and we will call..."

"How long?" I interrupted.

"Usually a week."

I nodded.

"Maybe two in your case, since it's Thanksgiving next week."

I nodded again, not daring to utter another word.

Then I had to go out, pay my deductible and wait while one of the receptionists scheduled my next appointment. I took my credit card out of my purse and started softly pounding it on the cold marble counter. The longer the receptionist took, while others around her scheduled other patients, the faster I began pounding my card on the desk until I wasn't sure I could stay any longer.

"I need to hurry," I told the young receptionist in front of me. "I got bad news today in there."

She took a look at my face and nodded. She moved the mouse of her computer with more urgency, typed faster and looked around, trying to grab the card payment machine from one of her colleagues but the colleague said the system was freezing and they had to try one more time.

I pounded my card on the reception desk faster and faster and the young receptionist looked at me apologetically.

My eyes filled with stingy tears and she saw me, so I stopped pounding my card, tried to think of something but nothing came to mind so I slipped my bank card to her and ran away.

When my mother found me, bank card in hand, I was sobbing uncontrollably in the middle of the hospital hallway. She put her arms around me and I noticed her eyes were full of tears too.

"Let's go home," she said, and together we walked out of the hospital to my car.

"Why don't you take the rest of the day off?" she asked me as I was driving her home.

"No," I said. "I need to go to work." *I need to be alone.*

As soon as I was alone in my car on the way to work, I started sobbing uncontrollably again. On the first street light I pounded the wheel of my car with open palms repeatedly.

Why? Why me? How can I have a child with Down Syndrome?

As soon as the thought crossed my mind, another one contradicted it.

How could I not?

I thought about my baby sleeping safely inside my womb. I then thought of a vacuum machine sucking the life out of it, pulling his little leg and yanking it off.

"Mommy, save me! Who is doing this to me?" I heard my baby cry.

"I am. I'm doing this to you. I don't want you."

The thought seemed so horrendous I knew I would not be able to live with myself.

I was going to have this baby, and I was going to love this baby because I already loved him. I became his mom as soon as I knew he was formed.

My two gold coins.

Still, I felt so ashamed. I felt ashamed of what others would think. Of me having been so proud thinking I could do this on my own.

Is God abandoning me? Is this a punishment for my pride?

Part of me knew it was pity talk. Part of me wondered if I had really gotten that permission from God or if I had defied nature.

If it had only been shame, maybe I would have gotten it out of my system sooner, but it wasn't only shame. I felt scared.

Will I be able to do this?

I cried at work all afternoon. I cried on my way back home. I cried myself to sleep for days and I cried as soon as I opened my eyes in the morning.

I don't know how I spent that Thanksgiving. I remember nothing about it other than waiting with a heavy heart for the weekend to pass so I could call the clinic to find out the results of my blood test.

By Monday morning, still praying to have a healthy baby, I had also resigned myself to the results.

I called the Perinatal office from work as soon as my Monday meeting was over. They had not received the results of my blood work yet.

I called again at noon. Still nothing. Near the end of the day I called a third time and asked them for the name of the diagnostic company they had sent my samples to. They provided the name and I looked them up online. I wrote down their phone number and dialed.

I explained that because of the holiday I had to wait over a week to find out my results and that I couldn't handle waiting any longer. A blessed soul answered my call, looked for the results and found them. She explained the results over the phone and I gasped as I wrote the numbers down on a post-it note.

I walked into my house that evening with the post-it still in my hand. From across the living room, my mother took one look at my red, swollen eyes and reached for the remote to turn off her soap opera, the smile vanished from her face as she opened a space for me to sit next to her on the loveseat.

"I got the results directly from the company," I explained in the best analytical voice I could muster. "Then I talked to one of the perinatals."

She grabbed the yellow post-it from my hand and looked at it but I knew she wouldn't understand.

"They're probabilities. One of my babies has a probability of a genetic defect of 1 in 8,000 and that is very good," I said and stopped to take another breath. My mom nodded and waited patiently for the rest. "My other baby has a probability of 1 in 98 of having trisomy."

My tears came out all at once and my mom hugged me, tears streaming down her face at my pain.

"Down?" she asked.

"No, and that's the worst part," I said between sobs. "Trisomy 13 or 18."

Mom's hand covered her mouth while I forced myself to finish the sentence.

"They said if I don't miscarry, my baby will die at birth."

Instead of drying her tears she covered my face with both her hands and wiped my tears.

"You will still have a baby to take care of," she said in the most tender voice ever.

I shook my head. "I feel like half my soul is dying."

That night while crying myself to sleep, I remembered the many times I had asked God for a baby.

"You can send me one from the adoption agency in Heaven, a baby no one else wanted."

Is this the baby no one else wanted? I'll take a baby with Down Syndrome, but please don't let my baby die.

Some days I thought that if my baby was going to live only while inside of me, then I had to give him the best possible life. I had to be happy, I had to eat well. Then there were the days when nothing consoled me. As the days turned into weeks my mother saw me crying in front of my bedroom and decided she couldn't take it anymore.

"Stop crying, love," she said and held me into an embrace again. "If there is nothing wrong with your babies, you will make them sick with all that crying."

Instead, I cried harder at her tenderness and patience. It always surprised me that my strong tough mother understood me best when I didn't understand myself.

She placed her hands on my growing stomach.

"I don't know what to do," I confessed. "I don't know if I should prepare for one baby or prepare for two."

Her face looked pained but then it changed.

"Have faith," she said, and I could tell she had been praying too. The words were so intense that a memory flashed before my eyes with the same intensity.

I was in a plane with my brother under bad turbulence and I thought we were going to die. Then I thought of angels holding up the wings and I knew there was plenty of time for the pilot to regain control.

Plenty of time.

The babies were inside of me, warm and safe in the right biochemical environment. There was plenty of time for them to develop fully.

I held on to that thought and although the worry never completely went away, my tears subsided. That evening I felt, for the first time, butterfly wings tickling inside of me. I asked my mom to go with me to Costco and I bought two car seats.

Eventually I also bought two cribs, and a darn minivan.

Many good things came from this experience. The first one was finding out how much I already loved my babies. I knew for certain I wanted two, no matter how difficult. From then on, when people told me,

"You have your hands full!"

I replied with a big smile. I felt lucky to have my hands full.

Also, I stopped mourning the life I didn't get to have. I stopped missing my romantic stories, because I knew for a fact that it hurt so much more to lose a child than to lose in love.

Chapter 20

NEW JOB

I WAS STILL in the middle of the IVF process when my boss at The Labs called all three of his postdoctoral scientists into his office. He talked to each of us individually, on the same day. I brought a brochure of a new UV Spec technology I had seen at my last conference. It had impressed me and I wanted to convince him of all the benefits it would bring to our lab.

"It requires only 10 microliters of sample and can run multiple tests at the same time." I continued explaining the benefits of this equipment over the old one we used in the lab. I spoke in a rush, nervous.

"It sounds great, but I called you into my office for a different reason."

Behind his back, I called him the Little Boss, because of his small stature and because he was only six years older than me, although I had great respect for him. Not only that, he was smarter than anyone else I knew. Plenty of times I had told myself,

By the time I am as old as that scientist, I will have enough experience to be as smart.

That didn't apply to the Little Boss. I doubted I would have his brains in six years.

This time, Little Boss seemed particularly serious.

"I have decided to take a new position," he said. "I can't take my current lab staff with me. I already told the other two postdocs they have to find new positions. You need to do the same."

What will I do? I asked myself as tears filled my eyes.

Before my surgery, I had received a rejection letter from the University of Texas. I cried at the missed opportunity but I had hoped to continue looking for a job while working at The Labs. Things had just gotten more complicated.

I did what I needed to do. I updated my resume. I called other researchers at The Labs who might be interested in hiring me, and interviewed with them. My two other coworkers found postdocs in different labs. One had to move to California, the other one was able to stay in Albuquerque.

I searched for positions within Albuquerque but the lack of biotechnology companies in the city made it hard for me to find a job. If I was willing to relocate I had better chances.

Then, as if meant-to-be, a position opened in Albuquerque for a scientist with experience conjugating antibodies with paramagnetic particles. I immediately applied, feeling sure I would get a call. Since I didn't get a call within a week, I applied again.

I soon received a message from a man named Viator Eichmann, the CEO of the company. He wanted to interview me and invited me to meet with him at a burger place, close to the company.

I dressed up in a suit and collar shirt, as expected for an interview. Upon entering the burger place, I removed the jacket but brought it along, just in case. At least it was a place I approved of. Their homemade bread smelled delicious.

He didn't tell me what he looked like, so I awkwardly waited for any signs that one of the few dozen men at the restaurant could be him. In contrast, Dr. Eichmann walked in and headed straight to me. He reached out his hand and I shook it the way one of my engineering professors taught me years ago, like a man. Dr. Eichmann was of medium height, medium figure. His most prominent features were his full head of white hair and the large nostrils on an otherwise sharp narrow nose, from which an abundance of untrimmed hair could be seen. He wasn't exactly cross-eyed, but the combination of sharp nose and close-fit eyes reminded me of a snake. Like my nightmares.

In my nightmares, I saw snakes crawling close to me. I moved to another room to evade them only to find myself surrounded by them again, on the floor and on the walls.

"I already ordered," I told Dr. Eichmann. "Please, go ahead," I said, pointing him towards the counter.

While he ordered, I selected a table, trying to find a place that wasn't too crowded. By the time he returned, my food had been served. I waited for his food to arrive to start eating, and meanwhile, I asked him questions about the company, then I let him lead the conversation.

"Have you ever worked for a Start-up company?" he asked.

"I have worked for different size companies, but not for a biotech start-up," I admitted. I had talked to people at The Labs who thought their best work experience came from working at a start-up. Many others, on the other hand, avoided them.

"We're a very small company but I am in the process of hiring at least two scientists for what will be the Immunology Department and a few engineers for designing the device. Do you know what NMR is?" he asked.

"It's a spectrum analysis," I answered.

"Right," he nodded. "We came up with the idea of using paramagnetic particles bound to antibodies to develop a diagnostic device based on magnetic resonance."

I nodded. Nothing new for me so far.

His number was called and he got up to get his food. When he returned to the table we both started eating.

"In theory, it will be capable of analyzing at the single molecule level," he said, sounding proud of his novel idea.

"Yes," I said. "I have been working with similar technologies." *I've done that already. The only new part is using it with your NMR detection.* I took small bites from my hamburger, trying not to get caught chewing when he asked his next question.

"It is hard to find someone with your experience in a place like Albuquerque. What brought you here?"

"The Labs," I said.

"I saw that on your resume." He sounded impressed.

We finished eating and stepped outside.

"I want to introduce you to other members of the company."

"Sure," I said and reached inside my purse for my keys.

"It's walking distance," he said, pointing to an area with some buildings across the street.

It was still uncomfortable for me to walk in heels after my surgery, but I did my best to suck it up and followed him. He introduced me to two other people, one of them a professor from the university who worked on the design of the device. They seemed cordial. The place where they worked didn't look professional.

"It's a temporary place," Dr. Eichmann explained. "We will be moving into a new location soon. It will be a better place."

He then asked me to meet with various people from the company. I arranged the meetings at their offices. Little Boss allowed me time to attend the interviews in the middle of the work day.

"The meaning of postdoc is looking for a job," someone said at one of the last conferences I attended.

I had a strong feeling I would get an offer. Like he said, my experience was very directly related with the company's goals. Although after working at The Labs, taking a job at such a small company felt like a huge step down. On the other hand, maybe that's what I needed. At The Labs I felt like I had climbed the ladder too high and it felt wobbly up there.

Then I received an email from Dr. Eichmann asking me for a second meeting, this one at his office at a start-up incubator building that belonged to the university.

He pointed to a chair in front of his desk and I sat down. I placed my leather bound agenda on my lap and took out my thinking pen.

"I can't afford to give you your current salary," he said. "I can offer you seventy five thousand."

I wrote down the figure on a blank paper, feeling relief the pay cut wasn't significant. I still hadn't learned the art of salary negotiation.

"You will be my highest paid employee in that department," he said and I believed him. Now I think all managers read that line from the same paperback book.

"I will not ask for a higher salary if I can get more vacation time." I tried my best to keep a poker face.

"How much vacation do you want?"

"From the attachment in your email it seems employees only get two weeks of paid time off a year. That's including vacation and sick leave. I want to be at the top level, which I believe is five weeks."

"Top level is for Directors and the Vice-President. I can offer you three weeks."

"That's not enough," I insisted. "We will be working with pathogens. Sick leave alone might be more than two weeks a year. At The Labs, we get sick leave separate from vacation, which is more than 3 weeks a year."

"We are a small company. I can't offer the same benefits you have at The Labs but I'm offering a comprehensive package. In addition to your salary, you will have stock options after six months. The health insurance is decent," he added, then looked at me. "You can add family members. Are you married?"

I knew that was an illegal question. "If that's important information, you will find out."

He nodded. "That's my final offer. Why don't you take a week to think about it?"

I rose from my chair. "That's a good idea. I will think about it." I had tons to think about.

I thanked him and returned to my work at The Labs.

"Why don't you wait another year to continue?" my father asked over the phone. "You need a permanent job."

My dad had tenure at the University of Puerto Rico, where he had worked for most of my life. He had also retired from the Army Reserve. I didn't know if those types of positions existed for anyone anymore, but they seemed to evade everyone in my circle. In graduate school no one told us what I termed the Gypsy Life, where as soon as you had gotten used to a place, or as soon as I had put curtains in my room, it was time to move. Staying in Albuquerque was the closest I could come to having some form of stability.

"Maybe you should've stayed in Florida," my father said.

I had loved working in Florida. "Dad, they might close the company there. The economy is bad. Everyone I worked with got laid off."

"What will you do?" he said.

"I don't know," I honestly told him.

It wasn't just me with big decision to make. One of my postdoc coworkers and her husband were trying to have a child. She found another postdoc in California, while her husband had to stay in Albuquerque for his job. My other colleague had just gotten married. She wanted to buy a new house. Now she also needed to think about it.

I interviewed at another national lab, about an hour and a half away from Albuquerque. For that position I would have had to work with radioactive material while pregnant. Between radioactive materials and biohazards, I leaned towards biohazards.

Meanwhile, I continued to administer my nightly injections. "I can always quit tomorrow."

At the end of the week, I knew my options were limited. Dr. Eichmann had said their health insurance was *decent*. A *decent* health insurance would not cover fertility treatments.

I either continue this round of IVF, or stop, not knowing when I'd be able to start again, if ever. I haven't gotten pregnant so far. Who knows if it will work this time at all. Quit or not quit?

I knew what I would regret more.

With some trepidation, I emailed Dr. Eichmann to let him know I accepted his offer, with the three weeks of paid time off. I would have to save every minute of those three weeks, and supplement with unpaid time off to give birth.

I signed the offer letter and brought it to him in person. "I am very excited to work with this new technology," I told him, and I meant it. Before leaving, I once again shook his hand, like a man.

When I got my positive pregnancy result and the six weeks ultrasound I still worked at The Labs. Around the time of my nine week ultrasound is when I transitioned to the new job.

My new coworkers and I got along immediately. They their cell culture protocols and how they charted the ability of the paramagnetic particles to bind to the pathogens. From there, I began implementing my own experiment methodology, which I believed improved over what they did. We worked in a borrowed laboratory from the university while Dr. Eschmann acquired the new building for our company, and shared the space with various other graduate students doing their research there.

We all discarded the used petri dish cultures in the same biohazard box. When it started to overflow, and I couldn't handle the disgusting accumulation of deadly bacteria anymore, I asked everybody to leave for the day while I disinfected the laboratory. The next day I instructed my coworkers on how to sterilize every surface.

That was the first day of work for a new-hire, Siri, a girl who had just finished her PhD in Chemical Engineering. She later told me she felt safe at work after she observed my sterilization procedures. I noticed Siri walked home after work and I started offering her a ride.

One day, as I drove her home, I felt a strong urge to tell her about my situation.

"I'm pregnant," I told her. "That's why I'm a neat freak at work."

"Really, Lani?" She started calling me that, after she heard it from my brother. She looked surprised, then relieved. "I'm trying to get pregnant too. I had a failed IVF and my husband and I are going to start trying again soon."

I stopped driving in the middle of the parking lot and looked at her. "Really? I did IVF. I'm expecting twins."

"That's wonderful, Lani! I want twins."

We found out we used the same clinic, although her doctor was Dr. Jameson's young partner. We both shared the same nurse and we agreed she looked like a beauty pageant contestant.

Siri and I became good friends. I became her IVF buddy, her cheerleader. She followed my advice and started looking forward to her injections. After her implantation, she stayed in my house because her husband had to travel for work. She looked so much younger and delicate than me. My mother and I took good care of her during that week.

Meanwhile, at work, my coworkers started telling me I was definitely showing. To me, I had been showing since I was 10 weeks pregnant, but my coworkers had bigger stomachs than me. In addition to Siri, I told a few coworkers but I hadn't told Eichmann. I wanted to wait until January, when I completed my first three months, the time that most companies considered you a permanent employee. At the company's weekly meetings, I used my lab notebook to hide my belly then sat in a way that the table covered my protruding abdomen.

By then, our department had four women and two men. The men, one in his late 20's and the other one in his early 30's, were wonderful. I trusted them with my news early on, and they always helped me with any heavy lifting. They moved my boxes when we had to move from the university building to our new site. When it was my turn to clean up the lab, one of them mopped the floor for me and took out the trash. In exchange, when it was his turn, I washed the glassware.

At our Christmas lunch, I wore a long scarf to cover my belly.

"I'm not sure that scarf is helping," one of my coworkers commented.

Then others joined the conversation.

"It's like using a tie to cover a basketball," Chip, the funny one of the two guys added.

"Maybe it's time to make your Big announcement."

"Really? They're all men, and engineers," I responded.

"Oblivious," one of them said and we all laughed.

Making the announcement at work was a common topic on the Single Mothers by Choice forums. Some women had it easy and had bosses who were supportive during the entire process. Some worked at schools and tried to coordinate their pregnancy so that they could give birth during the summer. Others didn't have it so easy. In fact, one of the articles I read before I started fertility treatments concluded that bankers and engineers had the hardest time getting pregnant. It had to do with the amount of support they received at work. To me, it felt forbidden, even though I felt less stress in this new job than at The Labs.

At this new job only one situation had scared me. After Siri arrived, we were given forms to fill out to apply for health insurance. One question asked if I was pregnant.

Why are they asking? It seemed so intrusive.

The next day, I showed the question to Dr. Eichmann's administrative assistant, who in addition to being the company's secretary also had the role of Human Resources department.

"You're not pregnant, are you?"

I was about eight weeks pregnant at the time. It still felt too recent and uncertain to me. Most women don't know they are pregnant at that point and the incidence of miscarriages was relatively high in the early weeks.

"I am, but I don't know…"

She looked at me, serious. "Don't know what?" She wasn't purposefully being insensitive, but it was clear she was busy and her mind was somewhere else.

"I don't know if I will *stay* pregnant."

Finally she looked at me, seeming to truly focus. She took the application from my hand and read the question. She shook her head. "Some people think they're entitled to information that is none of their business." She whited-out my check mark and marked the "No" box with a big check mark, put the application in a folder with all the others and left it neatly on top of her desk.

I felt relief. I had never considered that pregnancy could be considered a pre-existing condition. Still, the fear was enough that I decided to continue paying my previous insurance through COBRA for the rest of my pregnancy and beyond.

When it came to telling my boss my Big news, I took the advice of other single mothers and wrote down the key points I wanted to communicate.

- ✓ I am officially announcing that I am expecting twins in May.
- ✓ I don't know how much time I will need to recover.
- ✓ I want to return to work after my leave.
- ✓ Will you allow me to return to my **current position** after my recovery?

Other single mothers emphasized "current position" because some companies try to demote women after they gave birth, thinking they are less competitive.

I brought the notebook with me, not to read from, but to make sure I had expressed all the main points.

I knocked on Dr. Eichmann's door. When he answered, I said,

"Do you have fifteen minutes to talk? If not, I can come back at a later time."

"I have time," he replied. "Please, come in."

I settled into one of the two chairs in front of his desk then waited for him to sit down.

"I want to officially announce I am expecting a baby, actually, twins, in May."

"Wow, twins!" he exclaimed, his eyes wide. He gave me a friendly smile and I felt encouraged to continue.

"I don't know how long it will take me to recover but I want like to return to work immediately after. Will you allow me to return to my current position?"

"First, congratulations! I suppose it will be okay for you to return. It's fine with me."

I let out a big breath and smiled, thanked him for his time and hurried out the door.

Chapter 21

WEEK 20 ULTRASOUND

WITH THAT RELIEF in mind, I had a wonderful Christmas and holiday season. I wore a red long sleeve maternity blouse that made my belly look especially round and added extra color to my cheeks. I felt beautiful as I posed with my mother next to our Christmas tree. My parents, brother and I went to church for Christmas mass and we all prayed that my babies be born healthy. Tears came to my eyes as I thought about the newborn baby Jesus and I asked him to take care of my babies. Among the first items I bought for my babies' room, was a golden crucifix. I chose it thinking of the Divine Child.

I also bought two crib bedding sets, one for a boy and another one for a girl, although I had told Baby Jesus that I just wanted my babies to be healthy, I did not care what sex they were.

"You choose what you think is best," I told Baby Jesus.

The Perinatals were open on December 31st, which worked out great because I had the day off, so I scheduled my 20 week ultrasound for that day. I hoped the technologist could determine the sex of my babies so I could start shopping for them. Since my family was all in Albuquerque, I invited them to the ultrasound: my parents, my brother and Kim.

The technician helped me onto the bed, prepared the machine then allowed my clan to come into the room. She lowered the lights so we could all see the monitor images better. She placed the dropper on my abdomen and then the ultrasound probe over the cool gel.

I smiled at the first sound of the babies' heartbeats and felt relief upon seeing them move. They appeared healthy and happy.

I heard sniffing in the room and when I turned I realized both my father and brother were crying with big tears falling freely down their faces.

"Why are you crying?" I asked them.

My brother pointed to the monitor and the doppler.

"I didn't know it would feel so real," my Dad chocked out. I remembered he had never been to an ultrasound before. Even with his expertise in the medical profession, ultrasounds didn't exist when my mother was pregnant with my brother or me.

"Are you ready to find out the babies' sex?" the technician asked.

"Yes, please, yes!" I answered. "I'm not leaving this room until I find out."

She laughed and moved the probe over my stomach as she focused on the monitor.

"Aha!" she said, pointing to the monitor. "Baby A is a boy!"

"A Prince Charming," I said, smiling. As much as I wanted a girl, I could not visualize my life without a boy either. I had chosen names for boys and for girls, so now I could start calling them by their names. "Baby A is Ricardo," I announced.

My father smiled. He knew I chose Ricardo after him and my grandfather, the two men who most openly approved of my decision to become a mother.

"We're really happy," my mother said as she came to my side, bent down and kissed me.

"Congratulations," the technician said. She moved the probe to a different angle. "Now Baby B."

"Girl," I heard my mother whisper.

"Girl," Kim echoed.

At that instant the doctor walked into the dark room and the technician pointed to the monitor. "What do you think?" she asked.

"Yes," he said. They both agreed on something obvious to them but not so obvious to the rest of us.

Then I saw it. Something definitely sticking out.

"Baby B is a boy," the technician declared and the doctor nodded. "Congratulations," she said again, looking from me to my mother and Kim.

"That can't be. Check again," my mother said.

"Mom!" my brother and I exclaimed at the same time.

"Baby B is Ian," I happily announced.

My brother looked at me and winked. "Like me," he boasted to the technician and doctor.

Two Prince-Charmings. It makes sense, I thought. *I love boys, I have always known how to be their best friend. Or God really wants me to learn to deal with men.*

Then, another thought crossed my mind. *Gosh, I should've given them a taller donor!*

We celebrated by going to lunch at a local restaurant then I had my first official shopping spree for my babies, my boys. We went to the baby department at Macy's and I bought almost everything I saw in blue. At least, everything I liked.

"The pink clothes look so much prettier," my mom kept saying.

My dad and I rolled our eyes at each other.

"There's nothing I can do about that, Mom!"

I felt happy about my two Prince-Charmings, but at the end of the week, when returned the pink crib bedding, I also felt the sadness of not having a little girl.

I wonder if the third embryo was my baby girl.

Chapter 22

HELLP

IN EARLY FEBRUARY I had a visit with Dr. Mendez.

"You made it to 28 weeks with twins!" Dr. Mendez sounded both surprised and proud, as if claiming my achievement. "Your twins are now viable, which means if you go into early labor, they have a better chance of surviving."

That seemed like a wonderful milestone but honestly, every week seemed like another giant milestone. At the end of each week I celebrated by reading about my babies' progress on the book my sister in law gave me and online sites like BabyCenter, but after the results from the genetic screening I had decided to remain blissfully ignorant. The possibility that one of my babies was not achieving his milestones scared me too much. I still prayed every day, and did my best to eat well, now that my cravings allowed more food choices over the nausea. I still had to be careful about what I ate. Greasy foods like pizza and brownies sent me to the ER twice with gallbladder stone problems.

My energy level was high enough for me to go to the mall and buy everything and anything my heart desired for my boys. I bought identical outfits, after I decided it was part of the fun to dress them alike. I tried a couple of coordinated outfits, in which the clothes were either of similar colors but different, or different patterns with the same color, but in the end I decided not to complicate my mind.

"If I like one outfit better than the other, how do I decide which boy wears the cuter one?"

I worried about bringing the boys home and suddenly having to ask them,

"Which one are you?"

My friend Annie was planning to travel to Indonesia and I asked her to bring back two baby bracelets with my boys' names engraved.

My mother had wanted to return to Puerto Rico, but after my genetic testing results, she decided to stay with me.

In early February my family celebrated my brother's 30th birthday by going out to dinner with a few of his friends and his in-laws. My mother and I bought my brother's favorite cakes, one dark chocolate and one Chantilly. The night felt a bit chilly and my boys kept moving around. While the waitress took everyone's order, I placed my mom's hand over my stomach. One of the boys suddenly kicked so hard he knocked my mother's hand out of the way and my mother screamed. The startled waitress stopped taking orders and everyone turned to stare, wondering what was wrong.

I laughed so hard! My mother, still wide-eyed, apologized then turned to my babies and scolded them playfully.

"Boys, take it easy on your mother!"

If anyone had told me at that moment that my boys were going to be active, or more to the point, hyperactive, I would have told them I already knew.

At work, things were great. In many ways it felt wonderful to work at the new place. I stayed so busy I often forgot I was pregnant, that is, except when my boys decided to play a football match in the middle of a meeting. I wished I could stop the meeting and share my experience but work was work.

I also had to rearrange my social life by basically eliminating it. Before we moved to the new building, while we still worked at the university lab, I used to sneak out to my car for lunch, eat fast and sleep for 30 minutes. That became harder to do when we all worked together in the new building. Someone could easily spot me sleeping in my car. Instead I tried to sleep at least 10 hours at night, so I could make it through the day without needing a nap. I had no time for anything else.

I spent most of my time inside the lab, rather than in the office. Work moved faster and more energetically in the lab. I dreaded the idea of anyone saying I spent too much time in front of the computer. Also, I felt thankful I had a job at all, with the economy the way it was in 2009, amidst the Housing Crash. Still, I constantly felt fearful.

"I'm going to get fired," I said to my coworkers every time I had to return to work late after an appointment or the two times I met my friends from The Labs for lunch.

Before I informed Dr. Eichmann about my pregnancy, he used to bring visitors into the lab and I would hear him boast,

"She's the postdoc from The Labs."

When I first announced my pregnancy, Dr. Eichmann instructed his new Administrative Assistant, a girl a few years younger than me, to ask if I needed any accommodations.

"Could I get a maternity lab coat?" We had disposable lab coats but even the large size would not close around my expanding midsection.

"Sure," she answered. She and I looked through some science catalogues and online together but soon came to the conclusion that such a thing didn't exist.

"Don't doctors get pregnant?" I wondered.

"They sell maternity scrubs. I can get you one of those," she offered.

Scrubs were not as practical for biohazards. I could wear a lab coat over my clothes and easily put it on and off. With scrubs I would have to change into them in the morning and change back into my street clothes at the end of the day. We didn't have a sterilizing company that did the laundry for us, like hospitals did.

I kept searching and finally found an empire-waist coat. It

looked short on the model but would cover me below my knees. I ordered one in a size larger than I presently wore.

The stares and comments around the company began to change. While some coworkers were nice enough to offer me popcorn when they popped some in the office microwave, others made unnecessary comments.

Chip, the funny coworker, came to me seriously. "The boss asked if my work was falling behind because of you. I wanted you to know. I told him that wasn't the case at all."

The boss he referred to wasn't Eichmann, rather, a new Director of Immunology who had been hired to supervise our work. The new Director had seemed nice and professional. He had brought his children to work once. His son went to high school and his daughter had just been accepted at ASU. She planned to major in Mathematics. I assumed that with a daughter in a male-dominated field, he would be more open-minded.

Also, Dr. Eichmann didn't introduce me anymore when visitors came to the lab.

"I never noticed how much discrimination against women there is in the workplace," I told my friend Chiara one night over a phone call. As an engineer, I imagined she must have experienced it too. In my career, I had known of fellow women being passed on for promotions, considered not-as-smart or being sexually harassed, but none of those issues had touched me personally. I had kept on climbing my own ladder. I had never felt so vulnerable until now.

"Ignore it," she advised. "You won't be pregnant forever."

Since I had perinatal visits in addition to my obstetrician's visits, I would sometimes be late to work. To make up the time, I stayed late until I finished. Many days, I would be the one to close down the office. The one time Dr. Eichmann saw me late at night still at work, his jaw dropped. He didn't like it, I could tell.

He won't make me feel ashamed. I smiled and pulled my chin up.

One time, I obtained exciting test results. Instead of telling my coworkers at our small group meeting, I kept the results to myself. I told the others I had finished my work but had not analyzed the results yet, which was partly true. I did this because one of our coworkers, the first one among us to be hired, assigned herself a seniority role. She insisted on presenting for the rest of our group. I didn't want her to present a summarized version for me. Also, she had no sense of hypothesis. She often ran experiments that didn't work and came up with unrelated conclusions.

At our Monday meeting, she presented for the rest of the group as usual, then looked at me. "Lania, do you have something to add, or you still haven't analyzed your results."

"I can present." I stuck my pen drive in the laptop. "Last week, I coated this antigen with paramagnetic particles and achieved a 109% binding, which means that all antigens are binding to a particle or more."

Dr. Eichmann's eyes grew wide. He smiled a sideways smile. Everyone else at the meeting applauded my results. They understood the significance. I had just achieved one of the milestones of our company. At the end of the meeting, Dr. Eichmann informed everyone that in order to save time, from then on, only our coworker with seniority would be presenting.

Three major events happened early that Spring. The first one came from the SMC forums. In an email, a single mother informed us that she had become buddies with another single mother who had recently developed HELLP before giving birth to her baby.

I had to look up what HELLP meant. It consisted of a series of conditions also referred to as Severe pre-Eclampsia. The conditions included: hemolysis, elevated liver enzymes and low platelet count.

The single mother with HELLP died at birth without meeting her newborn son.

The news left me in shock. I couldn't imagine anything more horrible. Later at work, I asked Siri to go out to lunch with me. I needed space and time to think. I needed to talk to someone about this, but although Siri sat in front of me for the entire lunch hour, I couldn't bring myself to tell her what had upset me. I could not speak out the words. I grew very silent that day and it lasted a few days.

The second event took place the afternoon of Siri's 6 week ultrasound. Weeks before she shared the news with me that her IVF had worked. This time she brought the first ultrasound pictures.

"Two! I'm pregnant with twins!"

I hugged and congratulated her. I felt so happy for her and grateful for the friend she had become to me and for the success of her IVF and for our shared story.

Unlike me, Siri found no reason to wait before sharing her Big news. She showed her ultrasound pictures to everyone at work, including Dr. Eichmann.

"I'm pregnant with twins!" she proclaimed in every office and every cubicle.

That takes me to the third event. I arrived at work early one morning. Earlier than most people in our department because our office was mostly empty. I sat at my desk and turned on the computer.

Siri quietly came into the office and stood behind my chair. I felt her presence and turned. "Dr. Eichmann wants to talk to us."

I froze. There was only one thing Siri and I had in common.

I grabbed my notebook and my thinking pen and followed her into Dr. Eichmann's office. Our new boss, the Director of Immunochemistry, also sat there, next to Dr. Eichmann's desk.

Eichmann stood. "Wait a minute. Let me get my assistant."

He left the office and returned immediately. He once again sat behind his desk. His assistant followed with a legal notebook and an office pen in hand. All three of us sat, waiting.

Eichmann pointed to Siri and me. "I want to know how much time you are planning to take off. This is a small company and I can't afford to have two engineers from the same department off on vacation at the same time."

My brain raced, trying to come up with an answer, but mainly, I saw this as a moment in which I should have a lawyer next to me, and since I didn't, I needed to be my own lawyer.

What would a lawyer say? My mind raced. *Quick, think quick.*

"Siri and I are three months apart. We won't be taking maternity leave at the same time."

Siri nodded.

"By the time she needs to leave, I will already be back."

He wasn't satisfied with my answer. In fact, he seemed annoyed by its logic. "The work in a small company has to continue. We have goals to reach or we won't be funded for the next phase. If any of the other engineers asked me at this time for a month off, I would say no. A month is too much time.'"

I knew why he used the words *small company*. Family Leave law applied only to companies with more than 50 employees. His company's roster listed between 20 and 30 employees.

Think quick, I told myself again. No one else seemed willing to utter a single word. It had to be me.

"What are you concerned about? Are you concerned our lab work is not getting done?"

Eichmann shrugged but instantly the new Director spoke up.

"No, we're not concerned about that. Our lab goals are being met." Of course, it wasn't in his best interest to look bad.

That answer worked in my favor too. I wanted to take notes, I knew it was important to take notes, but at the same time, it was crucial to be thinking instead of writing. Still, I couldn't think of anything else to ask or say to our advantage.

"I haven't been told how long it will be. All I know is I will need time to recover from a C-section." *Eichmann couldn't be so cruel as to deny us the time to recover from a major surgery, could he?*

"Me too," Siri said, finding her tongue at last.

"Well, then. Let me know when you find out." With that, he dismissed us.

I grabbed my notebook and went back to the office. I tried to focus on work but couldn't, so I turned off the computer and went into the lab. I knew I had work to do but I couldn't remember what. My hands felt shaky.

I can't think, but if they don't see me working, I'm in worse trouble.

I went out in search of Siri. I needed to find out what she and Eichmann had discussed before I arrived. What had caused that meeting? She wasn't in our office and she wasn't in the ladies restroom. I saw her near the entrance to the building, talking on her cell phone. I tried to interrupt, but she asked me to hold.

Hold? What will I do until then?

I went into the secretary's office and saw her busy with paperwork but I interrupted anyway. "What was that?" I asked her in a whisper. "Does that mean we won't have any maternity leave?"

She smiled and shook her head. "I saw you during the meeting and I knew that's what you were thinking, but of course not," she said. "He only wanted to know the details."

I felt somewhat relieved. She also was a young mother who had to bring her 2-year-old son to work on occasions. She would probably want to have more children at some point. Still, she wasn't the one pregnant at that moment.

I went back out and Siri was still on the phone. The coworkers who had arrived were already in the lab, so I went back into our office and turned the computer back on. Since I couldn't focus on anything else, I wrote an email to the Single Mothers, press sent and turned the computer back off.

When Siri was able to talk, she explained she had been on the phone with her husband and a lawyer. When Eichmann hired her, he had told her he would sponsor her work visa, but all of a sudden he changed his mind. The lawyer had asked for a meeting with Eichmann and she had informed him that morning. That's when he asked to meet with both of us.

I waited to see if Eichmann would make an announcement to the rest of the company about his new leave policy. If the policy applied to the entire company, that meant that anyone who suffered a heart attack or a car accident, and needed more than a month off, was out of luck, but his announcement never came. Apparently the policy applied only to Siri and me.

Somehow I got through with the day and went home. I checked my email messages and had several from different single mothers.

"That's illegal..."

"Work discrimination…"

"No judge in Maryland would let him get away with that…"

They all reached the same conclusion: "Talk to a lawyer!"

I told my mother about my situation at work. "Can you believe that sonofabitch!"

I felt agitated all evening. I kept rubbing my stomach. Then I felt a strange twist of my skin.

"Is this a contraction?" I placed my mother's hand on my belly.

"Yes, that's a contraction," she said. "Is that the only one, or have you felt more?"

"I don't know," I told her, feeling around, trying to find my babies.

"If you have more tonight, we have to go to the hospital."

"Shit! Just what I needed. I can't spend the night at the hospital and have to take off tomorrow."

"It's your babies!" my mother said.

I went to the hospital and because I was more than 20 weeks along, they passed me directly to the Labor and Delivery unit instead of having to go through the Emergency Room. The doctor on shift determined I had mild contractions, similar to Braxton Hicks. He instructed me to see my OB the next day.

Dr. Mendez placed probes on my abdomen that reminded me of cardiac shock defibrillators. He also concluded they were Braxton Hicks.

"I want to see you more frequently from now on, and the Perinatals will want to see you more often too."

"I can't. I need to work."

"You have to start thinking about what's more important to you, work or your children," Dr. Mendez lectured.

"I'm going to get fired!"

"You made this decision by yourself. No one forced you. Now you have to be responsible for them."

I nodded.

"You don't have to worry about contractions until you're gripping with pain," he said and sent me home.

I returned to work.

At work, the subject wasn't brought up again, until I had a technical meeting with the new Director. He had praised my work and record-keeping in my lab notebook before.

"I want to keep my position," I stated after we finished talking about research. "I won't be pregnant forever."

He shook his head. "If you wanted to be pregnant, you should have gone to work for a large company or Academia, not for a small company."

I thought having a daughter in Mathematics would make him more sympathetic. I guess I was wrong.

Chapter 23

NATURE'S CRUEL WAY

I TOOK THE two car seats to the fire station so they could properly place them in my car. I drove an Explorer Sport, which basically means my car had 2 doors instead of the usual 4. I knew what my mother would say before I showed her the result. I had seen the struggle of the fireman putting them in.

"How are you going to place your babies in there?" my mother asked.

I had to push the seat forward and climb in the back while holding a baby and then turn the baby at an angle while I myself stood at an angle. It wasn't going to work. I had been looking at 4 door cars but so far I hadn't found the price I wanted on a larger SUV.

On Sunday, after mass, my mother convinced me to drive to the Honda dealer across from church.

"Hondas are pricey," I told my mom. I had already visited Ford, Dodge and Chrysler by myself.

"Let's just take a look," my mother insisted.

My father and I knew what it meant when my mother or brother uttered those words.

"Mom, I'm going to get fired."

"No, you won't. They would've done it already."

My mother shopped around for cars in a different way than I did. She wanted to look at them. When the seller offered a test drive she immediately said yes. She drove because I couldn't fit behind the wheel anymore. If I pushed the seat back enough to accommodate my stomach, then my feet would not reach the pedals. Since my contractions started, my mother insisted on driving me everywhere. In the afternoons, my brother picked me up from work.

In the dealership, she became best friends with the seller, a man at least a decade older than her, who looked like the Colonel from Kentucky Fried Chicken. With my mother's and the Colonel's help, I climbed in the back seat.

I touched the top of my stomach, which felt completely twisted to the side, like the Tower of Pisa. This felt much stronger than the Braxton Hicks I had a couple of weeks before. I had been feeling them since the previous Friday when the nurse placed the monitor on my abdomen and went to talk to Dr. Mendez.

The nurse returned to me and unhooked me from the machine. "Dr. Mendez says he's aware of your contractions. He says he already told you when to call him."

I nodded. No gripping pain on Friday so I went home for the weekend. No gripping pain on Sunday so I went to mass. The contractions felt stronger and more frequently, but I still wasn't gripping with pain. Not like in the movies. I could feel each one of the contractions and I had learned to predict when the next one was coming but no gripping, so I let my mother test drive the minivan.

The driver showed my mother the new technology that had come out for 2009. You could complete a total U-turn rotation without having to back up.

"That could come in handy with my driving," I said from the back seat.

The Colonel laughed and my mother peeked at me through the rear view mirror. She saw me hold my breath and hold on to the seat.

"Are you having contractions?" she asked.

I shrugged and nodded.

"Let's head back," my mother said.

The seller turned to look at me and agreed. Back in his office, he saw I was about to thank him and head out, so he wrote a number on a piece of paper and handed it to me.

I looked at it. $26,000. Even. That was how I bought a car. No test drive needed.

"Out the door price?" I asked him.

He nodded. Unlike other dealers, we don't work for commission here. We look for customer satisfaction.

Yeah, yeah, I thought. I had already shopped around for loans and had been pre-approved for that amount with the best interest in town. "Can you get the paperwork done in less than one hour?"

"I will get you out of here with your new car before your mother has to rush you to the hospital," he promised.

Once home, with a new car, my mother got on my case.

"You need to call your doctor."

I felt too tired. "I just want to rest. I'm not gripping with pain yet."

I could not sleep that night. Not because I felt worried about my new expense but because the contractions didn't let me.

In the morning, I called Dr. Mendez as soon as I knew he would be at work.

"What can I do for you?" Dr. Mendez asked.

"I couldn't sleep last night. I'm having contractions every two to three minutes."

"Then you must come over immediately. How soon can you get to Triage?"

"I can get there in 15 minutes but I want to take a shower…"

"If you're having contractions every two minutes, you won't be able to take a shower!"

I took a shower, then headed over to the hospital with my mother.

Once there, a nurse hooked me up in the now familiar equipment to monitor contractions. She looked at the recordings.

"Dr. Mendez asked me to call you if you had more than two

contractions in five minutes," the nurse said. "You haven't been recording for 3 minutes yet and you've already had two major contractions. Hold on here, I'm going to call him."

My mother took a peek at the monitor, which I couldn't see from my position. "Wow, those look like roller coaster waves. You're not in pain?"

"I can feel them, but it's not as bad as my menstrual cramps." I felt a tingling feeling over my cheeks before each contraction. "I can feel the next one coming."

Sure enough within a second my mother held her breath. "It's recording a huge wave!"

The nurse returned pushing a silver cart with an IV bag and injectable medications. "Dr. Mendez is on his way," she said. "I will get the IV going while he gets here."

Dr. Mendez ordered IV medications that stabilized the contractions. He showed up later.

"Good to see you," he said, friendlier than he sounded that morning on the phone. "You had me scared."

I lay on a narrow bed in the middle of the room with both rails up. My stomach felt so big that I feared falling if I moved to either side, so I sat as still as possible.

My mother sat on a chair next to me.

"Dr. Mendez," my mother said. "You mentioned a steroid injection to mature the babies' lungs."

"There's plenty of time for that. She's at 30 weeks, we're going to control the contractions to try to bring her as close as possible to 37 weeks, which is considered full term for twins," he said. "I'm sending her home today on Terbutaline to control her contractions." He turned to me.

"I'm ordering home rest, which is less restrictive than bedrest. That means you can stay at home and you can get up to use the bathroom or eat, but then you have to return to bed."

"But Dr. Mendez, I have to work."

He shook his head. "I can send you home or I can send you to the hospital on strict bed rest until you deliver. It's your decision."

Not the hospital, I thought. "I need to tell my boss."

"You can call him."

"I need to at least go in person. I will go early tomorrow but only to tell him and then I will go home and get in bed. I promise."

"Okay, but not longer than an hour. I don't like those contractions. You should've called yesterday."

"You said gripping with pain," I reminded him.

He nodded. "What I meant was...most women with those contractions...well, you call us. We have to make sure you're okay."

Terbutaline made me shaky. It's not given to pregnant women anymore to regulate their contractions because research has found it causes autism in babies. Back then, I felt very nervous about taking this medication. I had never taken asthma medicines so the jolting experience felt unique. My heart wanted to burst out of my chest. When I spoke, my words sounded as if I were shivering. In this state, I showed up at work Tuesday morning. Since I had been absent the previous day, Chip, Siri and my other coworkers surrounded me to ask how I was.

I shrugged. "I'm okay, but my doctor put me on bed rest."

All eyes grew wide and some of them inhaled deeply. They knew I was walking on a tightrope.

"I need to tell Eichmann."

"He's meeting with the engineers," Chip said, pointing towards the cubicles.

Eichmann was talking to one of the new device engineers. I didn't want to interrupt in mid-conversation, so I stood next to both of them, waiting for an opportunity. Eichmann looked at me in passing but chose to ignore me. The Director of my department saw me and I took the ungranted chance.

"Dr. Eichmann, I need to speak with you."

He looked at his watch. "I'm in the middle of something now. I can meet you after lunch."

I looked at the large clock in the middle of the office. *That's in 3 hours.*

The director intervened for me. "I believe she means now. Will it take long?"

"No, I won't take more than ten minutes," I said, hopeful.

Eichmann nodded and the director and I followed him to his office. He sat behind his desk and we sat in the two available chairs.

Eichmann crossed his hands on top of his desk. "Well?"

"My doctor said I had to go on bed rest."

Eichmann sat back. "And how long will that be?"

"Until I deliver."

He shook his head. "How long is that?"

"I'm due to deliver in seven weeks but…"

He hissed.

"But I think it will be sooner. I would really like to return."

Eichmann shook his head again. "You will change your mind after you give birth. My wife did."

"That's not an option for me," I assured him.

"All women change their minds after the baby is born. You'll see."

Eichmann said he had another meeting to go to and stood up to leave.

I left the company, hoping and praying their hearts would melt and I had a job to return to.

At home the days stretched in a way they had not stretched at work. My only outings were to the doctor and the perinatals. Even then, walking had become a challenge. Every time I walked, I felt Baby A, Ricky, wanted to come out, so I walked around the house grabbing my lower extremity.

"I feel like a whale!" I complained by email to the SMC group. "I can't get out of bed. I need to roll myself out."

Brooke shared the same feelings but she had gone into labor in January. When her time came, she was hilarious!

"My water broke and I'm not ready. I put a towel between my legs and I'm rushing around the house trying to pack a bag."

"How are you getting to the hospital?"

"My parents are coming to get me."

I had packed my bag early with everything I wanted for my twins, including their take home outfit, which my mother had ordered from my hometown. It came with cute matching blue baseball hats. My brother had placed the bag in the car the first time I had contractions and then moved it to the new minivan. I had to admit, the car seats fit much better in the middle seat of a minivan than in the back seat of my single-girl SUV.

Brooke had sent me pictures of her newborn twins right after birth. I could easily tell which baby was the boy and which was her girl. I couldn't wait to see mine.

Nights became more interesting when I stopped sleeping. I would feel tired and go to bed by 9pm but would wake up before midnight with only a couple of hours of continuous sleep. Initially, I thought it was my nerves and the meds but other single mothers said they had experienced the same thing.

"It's nature's cruel way of preparing you for what 's ahead," one of them wrote.

Now I had long days and even longer nights of wait. I decided not to get overwhelmed by sleepless nights. Instead, I got up, changed beds and grabbed my laptop.

I used my waking hours for researching work discrimination laws and contacting lawyers. I also used this time to get in touch with friends from different parts of the world with whom I had little contact due to work, time zones and distance. My international friends replied immediately. My local and Puerto Rican friends answered the next morning.

I got very interesting insights from some of my friends, mainly my friends from high school.

"You can't afford to be so picky with men," one of my closest friends said, before I told her the news.

"I will be as picky as my Princess-ass demands!" I retorted. "I can always choose artificial insemination."

"You said that in high school."

"I said what?" Now I had to stretch my arms to reach the keyboard.

"That you believed in artificial insemination."

"I said that?" It sounded like something I would say to shock my small-town friends.

Another friend, a guy who knew me since elementary school said, "I'm not surprised you chose to be a mother on your own. I would be surprised if any of the other girls in our class had done it. It was part of your personality."

I thought that was the sweetest thing anyone could say.

Then another friend who had come out of the closet recently, although I had never suspected it. "We were making a Punnett square in Biology class and you said you preferred artificial insemination so you could make your own choices."

"In Biology class? In front of the teacher?"

"No, the teacher was out of the room. Otherwise all of Moca would have heard about it instead of just your wide radius of friends. Like the time you confronted our homeroom teacher when he canceled our Halloween party."

"Yikes, that one got me in trouble when my father heard about it from his coworker." My father had been mad, but only until I explained to him why I had to speak up. He decided I was right.

"And the time you announced in class you were Pro-Choice."

I laughed, remembering everyone's faces, then I quieted down, hoping not to wake up my mother in the next room.

"Or the time I got pissed-off at the boys and told them they were afraid of women becoming more successful than them. We were taking an exam and the teacher took the exams from us and tore them all up."

"You loved stirring shit," my snappy-gay-friend concluded.

How could I have forgotten? Still, I wasn't trying to stir anything. I only claimed my own rights.

Then my paternal aunt made things clearer. I was afraid of what some of my family members would say, so in her case, I told the news of my pregnancy to my younger cousin and I allowed her to explain details to her mother.

My cousin reported back what my aunt said.

"She always said she wanted to be a single mother but I thought she would grab her boyfriend and knock herself up."

"So did I," I said to my cousin in reply.

That was my best explanation. At some point in my 20's as I fell in and out of love, I thought I would get married, as long as I could choose someone I loved and someone who would be a great father. I had a right to choose. Since I didn't meet that someone, I instinctively knew I could do it on my own. It was still my choice.

A little glimmer of light turned back on inside me, a light I hadn't realized had almost faded. It felt good to search deep inside me and rekindle my unique spirit.

Thinking back, I realized I knew I wanted to be a single mother since I was ten. I had a doll I loved and I wanted her to be real.

On Saturdays, I went to Catechism. We had a final test for Communion class. While other kids kept on going to Sister Maria Helena with questions, I answered everything by myself. I knew the answers by heart. Then I came upon the last question.

"When you grow up, how will you live life as a Catholic?"

I wondered if that was the question the other kids had problems with, but I knew I could answer it too.

I wrote, "I will raise my children in the Catholic faith and take them to church every Sunday with me and my husband."

What if I don't get married? Is it pretentious to assume I will? I felt sure I wanted children, but when I tried to imagine a man sitting next to me at church I couldn't picture it. In the end, I erased the words *"and my husband."* I turned in my exam, praying the nuns would not notice the omission.

By week 32, I felt so uncomfortable I couldn't wait to give birth. I went to my now weekly appointment with Dr. Mendez. Laying down on my back became nearly impossible. It made me faint.

"It's the babies' weight on your aorta. It cuts circulation to your brain," Dr. Mendez explained. "Hold on just a second," he said as he measured my belly with a measuring tape. He then helped me get on my side. To get to my side, I had to hold on to my heavy stomach and move it with me.

"How much am I measuring?" By now I knew that every inch of circumference represented one week of pregnancy.

He looked back on his chart. "You're measuring the equivalent of 43 weeks."

"Wow, they're big, aren't they?"

"They're growing, but you're small. There's not much place for them anymore. They probably won't be much bigger than five pounds."

"I know. My mother warned me a few weeks ago." *She freaked me out.* "I started eating more."

"Good," he said.

I had to call him early the next day.

"I'm itching all over my body. I can't stop scratching. The itching didn't let me sleep." My mother tried rubbing calamine over my arms and legs, palms and feet, but the itching never went away.

"I'm going to order some labs. Get them done today and I will call you back."

I did the nearly impossible task of getting dressed. I gave up on putting on socks and shoes. My feet had grown from a size 7 to a size 9. My mother had helped me get an open pair of sandals, the only ones that fit me at the store with the swelling on top of my feet.

"After I'm done with them, Abuelo can wear them," I said.

"Quit it, you have very cute pregnancy feet," Kim insisted. I loved her. My brother had proposed to her in the middle of my pregnancy and they had moved in together. They lived 5 houses away, so I still got to see them every day.

I got to the lab, got my blood drawn, then went home and collapsed on the sofa. My classical style uncomfortable sofa turned out to be the most practical thing for pregnancy because of its high armrest, which served as a backrest for me. When I wanted company, I stayed there with my cute swollen feet up, claiming the entire sofa for myself.

Two hours later, Dr. Mendez called.

"You have Cholestasis of Pregnancy," he said. "I'm sending some meds for you to take. It will help with the itching. When is your next appointment with the perinatals?"

"In two days," I said.

"I want to know what they say and I will talk to you."

Chapter 24

WEEK 33

I WOKE UP with contractions the day of the perinatal appointment. I kept taking Terbutaline but its effect didn't last long anymore.

"You can increase the dose, or take it every 2 to 3 hours," said the doctor who saw me that day, this time a woman. I never remembered any of their names.

They still made me get up on their examination beds, which I considered a safety hazard. She had to help me get down.

"When do you think I will give birth?" I asked.

"You're at 33 weeks?"

"Yes, today," I answered.

"Ideally, we would try to get past 35 weeks, but with those contractions, I think it will be sooner."

I sat on the office chair, a much safer option, and she took my blood pressure.

"Humm," she said, looking at it. "How much is your pressure normally?"

"Around 100 to 110."

She double checked on her chart and wrote down the current pressure.

I hated that they kept the numbers to themselves, so I turned to look at the sphygmomanometer. It read 135.

"Have you given us a urine sample?" she asked.

"Not yet."

She gave me a sample cup and the usual instructions, which I had down to an art.

I went into the tiny restroom, peed in the cup, closed the lid and placed it on the designated counter. A nurse came in and placed a strip in it.

"Please, follow me," she said and took me back to the examination room.

"How was the urine?" the lady doctor asked.

"She has 1+."

"Really?" the doctor responded.

"I have protein in the urine?" I asked.

"Yes. It's not a high level, but given that you've never had any before, I think we should inform your doctor."

"He wants to hear from you." Talking left me out of breath so I kept it to a minimum.

The doctor then looked attentively at me. "How are you feeling, in general?"

I stared back. I opened my mouth but couldn't find the words. Instead, I raised my hands, palms up.

"You feel heavily pregnant, huh," she answered her own question, laughing. "Did Dr. Mendez test your liver?" she asked.

"I'm not sure, but I have Cholest-aisis," I had trouble pronouncing it.

"Cholestasis of pregnancy?"

I nodded.

"I need you to get some labs and I will share the results with your doctor."

My mother walked with me to the lab. She held me by my elbow. When no one was around, I held on to my crotch. Unfortunately, one of the young phlebotomists saw me.

"You shouldn't be walking at this stage," she said and went to get me a wheelchair.

I saw heaven when she wheeled me around and didn't let me get up anymore. She drew my blood herself, took care of my paperwork and wheeled me back downstairs to the front of the hospital. We had paid valet parking and while we waited for the car, my mother took a picture of me and my 43 inch belly in the lobby of the hospital. I did my best to smile.

My mother shook her head looking at me. "Incredible."

The next morning I heard my phone ring around 8am but I had fallen asleep around 6am, so I completely ignored it. It rang again at 9am and it rang more than once, so I grumpily answered.

"This is Dr. Mendez. I've been trying to call you."

"I just fell asleep," I said.

"I can imagine. I need you to come to the hospital for an emergency C-section."

"Now?" I asked.

"Yes, now. No showers. Just get here."

I called my mother to wake her up. While she downed her coffee, I took a shower and washed my hair.

God knows when I will wash my hair next. I was right. It was ten days before I had another chance to wash it.

Kim arrived and helped my mother get me dressed and blow dry my hair. My brother said he would meet us there. Days earlier I had handed my brother the list of people to call or text once the babies were born. Kim said she would help him do that.

Coincidentally, my father had planned to attend a professional conference in Albuquerque. My brother had to pick him up at the airport later that evening.

Kim drove my mother and me to the hospital in my minivan. As we drove, it started to snow, big chunks of snow in mid April. My eyes got watery with happy tears. Every time I told my boys their birth story, I would start with,

"It snowed on the day you were born."

We arrived at the hospital at noon. A nurse greeted us in the maternity unit.

"Everything is ready for you. Dr. Mendez said we should call him immediately."

She led me to a tiny room and left us alone. Once again, my mom and Kim helped me undress and get into the hospital gown. This time, I had zero concern for my pride. Instead I felt pure panic and terror.

I got them in there, now they have to come out. I was about to be sliced open while still conscious.

The nurse gave me no time to ponder. She knocked on the door before we were done. She walked in with an IV while my mother and Kim helped me onto the bed. One of the perinatals walked in while the nurse plugged electrodes to different parts of my body. Because of the small space, my mother and Kim had to step out.

I remembered this doctor. He was the young one, the one who had given me the bad news about my baby's genetic condition.

"I thought Dr. Mendez was going to be here," I said.

"He's on his way," Dr. Bad news said. He carried a thick chart in his hand. "I'm here to explain some results to you. What has Dr. Mendez told you so far?"

On my left side, the nurse tied a rubber band around my upper arm and I winced at the tightness. She felt my arm for a good vein.

"He said I needed an emergency C-section."

"That's right," Dr. Bad news agreed. "Yesterday your blood pressure was high. It wasn't too high, but it wasn't only your blood pressure."

The nurse counted to three and poked my vein but couldn't find it.

Dr. Bad News continued. "Your urine sample contained protein."

"Yes, I remember," I said, as the nurse felt around my arm again for a better vein.

"Your blood results yesterday showed you had elevated hepatic enzymes and low platelet count."

The nurse tried to poke again but I withdrew my arm.

"Wait, please. I need to listen."

The doctor waited while the nurse agreed to wait.

I looked at the doctor. "Are you saying I have HELLP?"

"Yes. And the best alternative for HELLP is to deliver your babies even if it's earlier than we would have liked."

I looked around. The nurse seemed more worried about complying with her instructions than empathetic about what the doctor said.

"Are my babies in danger?"

"We have a wonderful team with you, including a team of neonatal doctors who will take care of your babies."

The nurse interrupted. "We have to hurry. Dr. Mendez is already scrubbing in the Operating Room."

The doctor left the room to allow my mother in while the nurse finished preparing me for surgery. She found a good vein this time and started the IV.

"What did the doctor say?" my mother asked.

I looked at her. "I have HELLP," I said in a trembling voice but I didn't get a chance to explain what it was or what it meant to me. A second nurse walked in the room and wheeled me away.

My mother held my hand until we got to the anesthesia room. At that moment, a nurse took her away to prepare her for the OR.

A new team of nurses helped me into a sitting position, with my back exposed.

"Try to relax," the anesthesiologist said as he tapped my spine.

Yeah, right, I thought.

After the anesthesia, they wheeled me into a second, wider room, where a new team of nurses and doctors introduced themselves. They all wore surgery hats, disposable robes, gloves and masks. Among them, I was introduced to my personal nurse, my babies' neonatal doctors and Dr. Mendez's associate. They moved around the room doing their tasks and talking cheerfully. I heard Dr. Mendez voice.

I tried to call him but I heard him say, "Tell her I have to keep this side sterile."

My personal nurse approached me with friendly eyes. "Are you nervous?"

I nodded and she held my hand.

"Ask her if she can feel this poke?" Dr. Mendez said and another nurse stood in the center of the gurney, as intermediary between the doctors and me.

I felt the poke on my lower thigh. "Yes," I said to the nurse.

"It's probably because she's nervous," the nurse holding my hand said.

They lifted the foot of the gurney so that my feet were higher than my head.

"Can she still feel it?"

I felt the second poke on my thigh. "Yes!" I said to the nurse.

"We only have ten minutes," I heard Dr. Mendez say.

Will he cut me open while I still feel pain? Is he that mad at me for being late?

"Hold on, sweetheart," the nurse holding my hand said. "I'm going to get your mother."

I squeezed her hand harder. "No. Let someone else get her."

The nurse stayed with me while they lifted the gurney further. This time I could feel my head considerably lower.

"I'm here, honey," my mother said. She took my hand from the nurse and sat close to me. She rubbed my hand with both of hers and whispered in my ear. "Take it easy."

"Now?" Dr. Mendez said and I looked at the nurse but didn't answer. She nodded towards Dr. Mendez and two seconds later came close to me and said,

"It's okay. He already cut open."

Soon after I felt a strong pull inside my body, around my upper ribs. My eyes grew wide. "I can feel that." *Is the anesthesia wearing off already?*

"Relax. He has to pull the babies out," my mother said.

I remembered my hippie doctor saying it took great strength to pull babies out, so I relaxed.

"Baby A is out," Dr. Mendez said. "Did you think about what you wanted to do?"

"Do everything you can!" my mother and I said at the same time. There was no way I was going to let him die next to me if all that was wrong with him was a bit of prematurity.

"I want to see him," I pleaded before they took him away. *What if this is the only chance I have of seeing him alive?*

The neonatal doctor took him from Dr. Mendez and on her way out, she showed him to me. He looked like a pink ball of skin with wet curly hair.

"Why isn't he crying?" I asked.

As if on cue, my baby cried and I felt a sob of relief on my chest. "Ricky."

The neonatal doctor took Ricky out of the room as Dr. Mendez pulled out my second baby.

Ian cried instantly. Dr. Mendez dictated the time of birth, like he had done with Ricky. Less than a minute had passed. Both my babies were born on the same minute. According to the clock on the wall, only one hour had passed since I arrived at the hospital.

The second neonatal doctor showed me Ian before taking him away. He looked just like his brother but skinnier. He also had wet curly hair.

"They got your hair," I told my mom.

It took much longer to get me out of the recovery room. Just like it had taken a while for the anesthesia to start working, it took awhile for it to wear off. The nurse in recovery kept asking me if I could move my feet or toes but I couldn't feel anything below my waist.

"The room upstairs is ready for you," the nurse said. "But we can't leave until you have some movement on your legs."

We had some long conversations between the nurse, my mother and I while I kept trying and trying to move my toes. As soon as I felt them move, I announced it and they sent me out to the next stage.

In the upstairs room, they exchanged my clear IV for an orange colored bag containing Magnesium Sulfate.

"This will help prevent seizures," someone said at some point.

Just looking at the orange bag made me nauseous but soon after, I was out.

Sometime in the middle of the night or day, my face felt hot. I tried to fan it with my hand. Someone brought in a fan and my mother placed a wet cloth on my face.

My mother went to see the babies and came back with pictures on her cell phone. She tried to show me a picture with Ricky's eyes open, but my eyes couldn't focus on it and I looked away.

I asked for something to eat and my mother tried to make me wait but I insisted. A nurse came in with a cup of jello. After two spoonful I moved my head away, then vomited. They let me be the rest of the night.

A group of doctors in white coats woke me up the next morning.

Mean people. I closed my eyes.

My mother answered the doctor's question but the doctor said she wanted to hear from me. I opened my eyes to stare at her with angry eyes.

How dare she talk to my mother that way?

The doctor insisted I needed to get up and walk.

I shook my head no.

"At least to the bathroom."

I opened up my eyes and looked at the bathroom door across the room. It seemed like a football field away. "Not strong enough," I said. My voice sounded hoarse. Not my own.

"For my daughter to say she's not strong enough..." my mother trailed off.

The doctor gave up and left the room in a bad mood but a nurse stayed behind, trying to sweet talk me into getting up.

I ignored her.

"Can you breathe?" she asked me.

What a stupid question. I'm not dead. I nodded.

"Take a deep breath," she said and placed her stethoscope on my chest.

I tried but realized I couldn't.

"Can you move your legs?" she asked.

I tried and nothing moved. I started worrying about my legs.

"How about your arms? Can you lift your arms?"

I lifted them but they barely rose above the bed.

"Let me talk to the doctor," the nurse said and left the room.

Good, I thought and closed my eyes again.

When I opened my eyes again, her face was inches away from mine.

"I'm removing your magnesium sulfate. It seems we gave you an overdose."

She must have stayed in the room for a while because she was still there the next time I opened my eyes.

"Good. Take a deep breath now." She once again placed the stethoscope on my chest. "Much better."

I smiled.

My mother placed a new wet rag over my face and the coolness felt good. "Do you think you can walk now?"

I looked at the bathroom door again and tried to move my legs. "No."

I suddenly felt an emptiness inside my chest. "I want to see my babies."

"Not if you can't walk," the nurse said. "The effects of the medicine should start fading in about an hour. We can try again then."

I looked around for a clock and found one above the bathroom door. One hour. I tried to wiggle my toes. Nothing.

Fifteen minutes later, while my mother and the nurse chatted quietly, I tried again and felt some movement but I didn't say anything. After half an hour I could move my legs. I kept watching the clock.

"I want to walk now," I said when the hour passed. They looked at me in surprise.

They helped me up and holding on to them I walked to the bathroom door but got dizzy and faint, so they sat me in a chair. I tried, though.

"I want to see my babies."

The nurse smiled and went to get a wheelchair.

To get into NICU I had to wash my hands like a surgeon before surgery. They took me into a room full of tiny incubators and frequently beeping machines. In the picture my mother tried to show me, Ricky looked chubby, but looking at him closely he looked tiny and delicate. I didn't recognize him as the boy they showed me during my C-section. For one, this tiny baby had straight hair. He had chubby legs and knew he would have my thighs. His lips looked very red and puffy.

The kissy lips of a doll, I thought.

I felt guilty for the huge IV needle inserted into the back of his tiny dime sized hand. To this date, I can still see the marks the IV left on both boys.

"My poor baby," I whispered.

A nurse came by. "This must be Mom," she said. "You can touch him."

She showed me how to insert my hand into the glove of the incubator and how to gently pad his skin instead of rubbing it.

"Where's Ian?" I asked.

My nurse wheeled me around and let my mother guide us.

Ian didn't look to me like his brother, although he also had straight hair. He had wide straight lips, a smaller nose. Actually, Ian looked even tinier, skinnier. I found out Ricky weighed 4 pounds with 3 ounces, while Ian weighed only 3 pounds with 11 ounces. I began to cry.

A lady with long white hair walked over and introduced herself. "Don't cry," she said and hugged me. "I volunteer because I had a preemie daughter myself and I'm here to tell you she is now in college doing great. Your kiddos will do well too."

Her words felt like the mustard seeds I needed. I wanted to stay longer but my nurse said I should come back later.

"You're in no condition to be out of your own room."

Back in my room, I went to the bathroom and saw myself in the mirror. I couldn't believe it was me. My face looked swollen and red, as if I had gotten a horrible sunburn. Later, after I became friends with the NICU nurses, they told me,

"You looked like you were not going to make it."

In fact, before I left the hospital, the skin on my face started peeling.

Some of my friends from The Labs came to visit and brought flowers and gifts for the babies. Siri also came to visit, all excited. I hadn't seen her in weeks and now she had a full round belly.

After they left I had another visitor.

"Papi!" I wrapped my arms around him.

"Congratulations, hija!" He said with a big proud smile.

"When did you arrive? Have you seen them?"

"He hasn't seen the babies but he came last night to see you," my mom said.

"Really?" I asked.

"I did and you greeted me," my dad replied.

"Really!" My memories from the last 24 hours felt blurry.

I went back to NICU with my dad and showed him my two baby boys. Some of the babies at NICU fit in the palm of a hand. My babies fit in two hands. They did wonderfully in NICU and every day they graduated to a new section.

I pulled every neonatology doctor to ask if either of my babies had Trisomy.

"No way!" they declared.

I pulled one and made her walk with me to their cribs.

"Genetic tests have a high chance of false positives," she assured me. "Your babies look perfect."

They passed hearing tests, blood tests and heart tests. They failed Occupational hyperactivity tests, but I already knew that.

"I can deal with that," I told the Occupational Therapist. Many years later, I encountered that same therapist again at a different time in our lives, when beeping machines became the norm again.

Dr. Mendez assigned me an extra day, for a total of 5 days in the hospital. The worst part was the day I had to go home while the boys stayed in the hospital 3 more weeks. I cried like they were tearing me apart.

"Postpartum depression," the nurses and doctors claimed and to my annoyance, my mother agreed.

I didn't feel depressed. I felt cold dread of being away from my babies. I missed them the moment I stopped feeling them move inside me. I feared getting a call from the hospital saying one of them didn't make it through the night, just like it happened to my second cousin, who had twins a year before mine. I knew I would never recover from that.

I resigned myself to driving home that day with two empty car seats. Every tiny bump on the road hurt, just like it happened after my first surgery. My father helped me out of the car and into my house. Once inside I sat on the sofa with my back resting on the high arm rest. I no longer had a round belly to rub, only a sore scar.

My mother brought a cup of juice and after a sip, she took it from me and placed it on the coffee table.

"We need to buy groceries. You stay sitting there until we're back. Don't go climbing the stairs."

I nodded.

As soon as they left, I walked up the stairs, holding to the railing and taking one step at a time, steadying myself before taking the next step. I walked into the nursery, which I had decorated with yellow wooden moon and stars on the wall and matching lamps on the dresser. My mother had sewn blue gingham curtains for the window. Lastly, I had decorated the two cherry wood cribs, gifts from my parents with the cream and green Pooh bedding sets I purchased when I found out I was pregnant. I had replaced the girl bedding for a Pooh set, identical to the first one. Even the double stroller sat there, waiting to be used.

Please, God, let them come home soon. Both of them.

When my parents arrived, they found me sitting on the sofa, in the same position they had left me. I had emptied half the juice.

I recovered from the C-section much faster than from my previous surgery due to my insistence of going to NICU every day for the next three weeks to spend the day with my babies. I would hold one all through the morning, and the other one all through the afternoon. I felt they still needed time inside me and since they were tiny, I fit them in the cleavage between my breasts.

The day before Mother's Day, I brought Ian home with me. I spent the morning of my first Mother's Day with Ian, and the rest of the day in NICU with Ricky. The day after Mother's Day, I brought Ricky home. They wore their handmade outfits of linen and bobbin lace. The house, their cribs, my hands and my heart felt full.

I learned to hold them both in my arms at the same time, where I paid close attention to their developing features. The one who looked the most like the donor, also looked like my brother. He inherited my almond shaped brown eyes. The one that looked the most like me, inherited the donor's blue eyes. I decided to place a picture of the donor in their bedroom.

"You were born from love," I constantly said to my babies and I still do. "Some children are born from the love between a man and a woman, but you were born directly from the love I felt for you."

My dad was able to spend some wonderful first days with us. "You think this is the end of your journey, but it is only the beginning," he said.

He could not have predicted it better, but that's an entirely different story.

EPILOGUE

"What looks like a loss may be the very event which is subsequently responsible for helping to produce the major achievement of your life." --Srully D. Blotnick

AFTER DR. EICHMANN met with Siri and me, I emailed my local SMC group. One of them referred me to the BioLaw firm, where I spoke to the most wonderful lawyer in the world. We planned to send a letter to my employer since she strongly believed we had a misunderstanding, but when I went on bedrest, my situation became complicated. It seemed my best option was to file a Discrimination Charge through the Equal Employment Opportunity Commission or EEOC. Eichmann received the filing on the day I gave birth. Siri said chaos ensued in the company on that day. All my coworkers, the ones I had overheard planning a baby shower, were forbidden to contact me. Only Siri defied the order.

On my way to NICU during the second week of my boys' stay, I received a certified letter from the lawyers representing Eichmann and his company. In the letter, the lawyers claimed I had abandoned my position. They claimed I had not given any indication that I wanted to return to work and thus I had no job to return to. That was clearly bullshit. I had seen a published posting for my position before I gave birth.

A 3 year long battle ensued and I wanted to take them to court, but my lawyers recommended we settle the case through a mediator.

At the end of the mediation I was asked if I was pleased with the results.

"My lawyer says that in a successful mediation, both parties come out feeling like they lost. In that sense, it must have been a successful one."

I lost my pretty townhome to foreclosure. I lost my high credit scores and my ability to obtain a loan and the lowest interest rate. In some ways, I also lost my career. I didn't fall from the ladder. I was pushed and I never again climbed as high.

Many times my mother saw me stare out into space and my silence told her what I was thinking.

"How will I manage to support my children now? How will I provide for them and give them their Christmas presents?"

Before my boys left the hospital, I bought them their first book at a sale in the hospital lobby. *I Knew You Could! A Book for All the Stops in Your Life*, from *The Little Engine That Could* series, by Craig Dorfman and Cristina Ong.

> You'll go through tunnels, surrounded by dark,
> And you'll wish for a light or even a spark.
> You might get scared or a little bit sad,
> Wondering if maybe your track has gone bad.
> So here's some advice to help ease your doubt:
> The track you took in must also go out.
> So steady yourself and just keep on going–
> Before you know it, some light will be showing.

As I read the book to my boys, my mother repeated some of the sections to me. Like an echo from the tunnel.

Looking back, not having a job helped me stay with my boys longer. I made them home-made organic baby food, while as a single mother, I had planned on using canned basics. Abuelo asked to meet them and because my father had a job to return to while I didn't, I traveled to Puerto Rico with my 4-month-old boys. Abuelo called them *los peluches*, his teddy bears. Abuela gave us our one and only Baby Shower in her house. We celebrated their first birthday at a pony farm, with my whole big family. It was the last family gathering Abuelo had with us.

If I had known, before I got pregnant, everything we were going to go through, everything I mention in this book and beyond, I would have frozen with fear. I might not have taken the steps I took. I also would have missed on so many more wonderful moments.

I don't regret my choice to become a Single Mother by Choice. Never for a second will I regret being the mother of my two Prince-Charmings. I would have regretted not having had them. I know this for sure, because I have come close to losing one of them, and the pain felt like the proverbial sword to the heart.

They are the best part of my life, my biggest dream come true. Every night when I get them in bed they ask for hugs and kisses. I still thank God for every day of their lives. I still feel wonder at how I got so lucky. They are by far, my most wonderful adventure.

ACKNOWLEDGEMENTS

THANK YOU ANNIE, Brooke, Siri, Chiara, Yari, Barbie, snappy Carlos and *comadre*, for helping me along the way. Thank you to all the friends who helped me through this process.

Thank you Ms. Gayle Wise. We will always remember our kindergarten teacher. Thank you for your continued friendship and for your amazing work editing this book.

This will be the third paragraph and fourth:

Thank you to my family. I have the best family in the world. I love you all.

Thank you Via, Yen, Peter and the Balboa Press staff who helped with my project. It's been a pleasure working with you.

Thank you Dr. Lyle Skains. You are the best Creative Writing professor and Book Slayer.

Thank you Karen McDonnell Hilligoss for your advice on publishing with Balboa Press and your motivation to finish my book.

Thank you Allen and Hubbell. You were two pieces of the puzzle. I have nice memories of our time in graduate school. You made it more fun.

Thank you Donor 11349, for the gift of life.

Thank you Ian and Ricky, for choosing the title and cover. Most importantly, thank you for choosing me to be your mother.

Thank you Baby Jesus for trusting me with two angels from heaven, and for sending them healthy into my arms. I am forever grateful.

ABOUT THE AUTHOR

LANIA SALAS WAS born in Puerto Rico and moved to Arizona to attend graduate school at Arizona State University, where she enriched many lives through her kind heart and zest for life. She currently lives in Albuquerque, NM with her twin sons. She continues to spread joy and love through her openness and acceptance of all.